Harvard
Business
Review

ON

BREAKTHROUGH

THINKING

THE HARVARD BUSINESS REVIEW PAPERBACK SERIES

The series is designed to bring today's managers and professionals the fundamental information they need to stay competitive in a fast-moving world. From the preeminent thinkers whose work has defined an entire field to the rising stars who will redefine the way we think about business, here are the leading minds and landmark ideas that have established the *Harvard Business Review* as required reading for ambitious businesspeople in organizations around the globe.

Other books in the series:

Harvard Business Review on Brand Management

Harvard Business Review on the Business Value of IT

Harvard Business Review on Change

Harvard Business Review on Corporate Strategy

Harvard Business Review on Effective Communication

Harvard Business Review on Entrepreneurship

Harvard Business Review on Knowledge Management

Harvard Business Review on Leadership

Harvard Business Review on Managing High-Tech Industries

Harvard Business Review on Managing People

Harvard Business Review on Managing Uncertainty

Harvard Business Review on Measuring Corporate Performance

Harvard Business Review on Nonprofits

Harvard Business Review on Strategies for Growth

Harvard Business Review

ON

BREAKTHROUGH

THINKING

A HARVARD BUSINESS REVIEW PAPERBACK

The *Harvard Business Review* articles in this collection are available as individual reprints. Discounts apply to quantity purchases. For information and ordering, please contact Customer Service, Harvard Business School Publishing, Boston, MA 02163. Telephone: (617) 496-1449, 8 A.M. to 6 P.M. Eastern Time, Monday through Friday. Fax: (617) 496-1029, 24 hours a day. E-mail: custserv@hbsp.harvard.edu.

Library of Congress Cataloging-in-Publication Data
Harvard business review on breakthrough thinking.
    p.   cm.—(A Harvard business review paperback)
    Includes index.
    ISBN 1-57851-181-X (alk. paper)
    1. Creative ability in business.   2. Technological innovations—Management.   3. Organization.   I. Harvard business review.   II. Series: Harvard business review paperback series.
HD53.H377   1999
658.4'06—dc21   99-18900
                                                                            CIP

The paper used in this publication meets the requirements of the American National Standard for Permanence of Paper for Printed Library Materials Z39.49-1984.

Contents

Harvard Business Review

ON

BREAKTHROUGH
THINKING

How to Kill Creativity

TERESA M. AMABILE

Executive Summary

IN TODAY'S KNOWLEDGE ECONOMY, creativity is more important than ever. But many companies unwittingly employ managerial practices that kill it. How? By crushing their employees' *intrinsic motivation*—the strong internal desire to do something based on interests and passions.

Managers don't kill creativity on purpose. Yet in the pursuit of productivity, efficiency, and control—all worthy business imperatives—they undermine creativity. It doesn't have to be that way, says Teresa Amabile. Business imperatives can comfortably coexist with creativity. But managers will have to change their thinking first.

Specifically, managers will need to understand that creativity has three parts: expertise, the ability to think flexibly and imaginatively, and motivation. Managers can influence the first two, but doing so is costly and slow. It would be far more effective to increase employees' intrinsic motivation.

To that end, managers have five levers to pull: the amount of challenge they give employees, the degree of freedom they grant around process, the way they design work groups, the level of encouragement they give, and the nature of the organizational support.

Take challenge as an example. Intrinsic motivation is high when employees feel challenged but not overwhelmed by their work. The task for managers, therefore, becomes matching people to the right assignments. Consider also freedom. Intrinsic motivation—and thus creativity—soars when managers let people decide *how* to achieve goals, not *what* goals to achieve.

Managers *can* make a difference when it comes to employee creativity. The result can be truly innovative companies in which creativity doesn't just survive but actually thrives.

W HEN I CONSIDER all the organizations I have studied and worked with over the past 22 years, there can be no doubt: creativity gets killed much more often than it gets supported. For the most part, this isn't because managers have a vendetta against creativity. On the contrary, most believe in the value of new and useful ideas. However, creativity is undermined unintentionally every day in work environments that were established—for entirely good reasons—to maximize business imperatives such as coordination, productivity, and control.

Managers cannot be expected to ignore business imperatives, of course. But in working toward these imperatives, they may be inadvertently designing organizations that systematically crush creativity. My research shows that it is possible to develop the best of both worlds: organizations in which business imperatives are attended to *and* creativity flourishes. Building such organizations, however, requires us to understand precisely what kinds of managerial practices foster creativity—and which kill it.

What Is Business Creativity?

We tend to associate creativity with the arts and to think of it as the expression of highly original ideas. Think of how Pablo Picasso reinvented the conventions of painting or how William Faulkner redefined fiction. In business, originality isn't enough. To be creative, an idea must also be appropriate—useful and actionable. It must somehow influence the way business gets done—by improving a product, for instance, or by opening up a new way to approach a process.

The associations made between creativity and artistic originality often lead to confusion about the appropriate place of creativity in business organizations. In seminars, I've asked managers if there is any place they *don't* want creativity in their companies. About 80% of the time, they answer, "Accounting." Creativity, they seem to believe, belongs just in marketing and R&D. But creativity can benefit every function of an organization. Think of activity-based accounting. It was an invention—an *accounting* invention—and its impact on business has been positive and profound.

Along with fearing creativity in the accounting department—or really, in any unit that involves systematic processes or legal regulations—many managers also hold a rather narrow view of the creative process. To them, creativity refers to the way people think—how inventively they approach problems, for instance. Indeed, thinking imaginatively is one part of creativity, but two others are also essential: *expertise* and *motivation.* (See the graph "The Three Components of Creativity.")

The Three Components of Creativity

Within every individual, creativity is a function of three components: expertise, creative-thinking skills, and motivation. Can managers influence these components? The answer is an emphatic yes—for better or for worse—through workplace practices and conditions.

Expertise is, in a word, knowledge—technical, procedural, and intellectual.

Creative-thinking skills determine how flexibly and imaginatively people approach problems. Do their solutions upend the status quo? Do they persevere through dry spells?

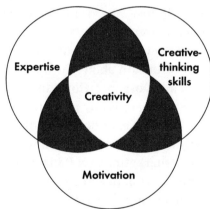

Not all **motivation** is created equal. An inner passion to solve the problem at hand leads to solutions far more creative than do external rewards, such as money. This component—called *intrinsic motivation*—is the one that can be most immediately influenced by the work environment.

Expertise encompasses everything that a person knows and can do in the broad domain of his or her work. Take, for example, a scientist at a pharmaceutical company who is charged with developing a blood-clotting drug for hemophiliacs. Her expertise includes her basic talent for thinking scientifically as well as all the knowledge and technical abilities that she has in the fields of medicine, chemistry, biology, and biochemistry. It doesn't matter how she acquired this expertise, whether through formal education, practical experience, or interaction with other professionals. Regardless, her expertise constitutes what the Nobel laureate, economist, and psychologist Herb Simon calls her "network of possible wanderings," the intellectual space that she uses to explore and solve problems. The larger this space, the better.

Creative thinking, as noted above, refers to *how* people approach problems and solutions—their capacity to put existing ideas together in new combinations. The skill itself depends quite a bit on personality as well as on how a person thinks and works. The pharmaceutical scientist, for example, will be more creative if her personality is such that she feels comfortable disagreeing with others—that is, if she naturally tries out solutions that depart from the status quo. Her creativity will be enhanced further if she habitually turns problems upside down and combines knowledge from seemingly disparate fields. For example, she might look to botany to help find solutions to the hemophilia problem, using lessons from the vascular systems of plants to spark insights about bleeding in humans.

As for work style, the scientist will be more likely to achieve creative success if she perseveres through a difficult problem. Indeed, plodding through long dry spells of tedious experimentation increases the probability of truly creative breakthroughs. So, too, does a work style that uses "incubation," the ability to set aside difficult problems temporarily, work on something else, and then return later with a fresh perspective.

Expertise and creative thinking are an individual's raw materials—his or her natural resources, if you will. But a third factor—motivation—determines what people will actually do. The scientist can have outstanding educational credentials and a great facility in generating new perspectives to old problems. But if she lacks the motivation to do a particular job, she simply won't do it; her expertise and creative thinking will either go untapped or be applied to something else.

My research has repeatedly demonstrated, however, that all forms of motivation do not have the same impact on creativity. In fact, it shows that there are two types of motivation—*extrinsic* and *intrinsic*, the latter being far more essential for creativity. But let's explore extrinsic first, because it is often at the root of creativity problems in business.

Extrinsic motivation comes from *outside* a person— whether the motivation is a carrot or a stick. If the scientist's boss promises to reward her financially should the blood-clotting project succeed, or if he threatens to fire her should it fail, she will certainly be motivated to find a solution.

Money doesn't necessarily stop people from being creative, but in many situations, it doesn't help.

But this sort of motivation "makes" the scientist do her job in order to get something desirable or avoid something painful.

Obviously, the most common extrinsic motivator managers use is money, which doesn't necessarily stop people from being creative. But in many situations, it doesn't help either, especially when it leads people to feel that they are being bribed or controlled. More important, money by itself doesn't make employees passionate about their jobs. A cash reward can't magically prompt people to find their work interesting if in their hearts they feel it is dull.

But passion and interest—a person's internal desire to do something—are what intrinsic motivation is all about. For instance, the scientist in our example would be intrinsically motivated if her work on the blood-clotting drug was sparked by an intense interest in hemophilia, a personal sense of challenge, or a drive to crack a problem that no one else has been able to solve. When people are intrinsically motivated, they engage in their work for the challenge and enjoyment of it. The work *itself* is motivating. In fact, in our creativity research, my students, colleagues, and I have found so much evidence in favor of intrinsic motivation that we have articulated what we call the *Intrinsic Motivation Principle of Creativity*: people will be most creative when they feel motivated primarily by the interest, satisfaction, and challenge of the work itself—and not by external pressures. (For more on the differences between intrinsic and extrinsic motivation, see "The Creativity Maze" at the end of this article.)

Managing Creativity

Managers can influence all three components of creativity: expertise, creative-thinking skills, and motivation. But the fact is that the first two are more difficult and time consuming to influence than motivation. Yes, regular scientific seminars and professional conferences will undoubtedly add to the scientist's expertise in hemophilia and related fields. And training in brain-storming, problem solving, and so-called lateral thinking might give her some new tools to use in tackling the job. But the time and money involved in broadening her knowledge and expanding her creative-thinking skills would be great. By contrast, our research has shown that intrinsic motivation can be increased considerably by even subtle changes in an organization's environment. That is not to say that managers should give up on improving expertise and creative-thinking skills. But when it comes to pulling levers, they should know that those that affect intrinsic motivation will yield more immediate results.

More specifically, then, what managerial practices affect creativity? They fall into six general categories: challenge, freedom, resources, work-group features, supervisory encouragement, and organizational support. These categories have emerged from more than two decades of research focused primarily on one question: What are the links between work environment and creativity? We have used three methodologies: experiments, interviews, and surveys. While controlled experiments allowed us to identify causal links, the interviews and surveys gave us insight into the richness and complexity of creativity within business organizations. We have studied dozens of companies and, within those, hundreds of individuals and teams. In each research initiative, our goal has been to identify which managerial practices are definitively linked to positive creative outcomes and which are not.

For instance, in one project, we interviewed dozens of employees from a wide variety of companies and industries and asked them to describe in detail the most and least creative events in their careers. We then closely studied the transcripts of those interviews, noting the managerial practices—or other patterns—that appeared repeatedly in the successful creativity stories and, conversely, in those that were unsuccessful. Our research has also been bolstered by a quantitative survey instrument called KEYS. Taken by employees at any level of an organization, KEYS consists of 78 questions used to assess various workplace conditions, such as the level of support for creativity from top-level managers or the organization's approach to evaluation.

Taking the six categories that have emerged from our research in turn, let's explore what managers can do to enhance creativity—and what often happens instead. Again, it is important to note that creativity-killing practices are seldom the work of lone managers. Such practices usually are systemic—so widespread that they are rarely questioned.

CHALLENGE

Of all the things managers can do to stimulate creativity, perhaps the most efficacious is the deceptively simple task of matching people with the right assignments. Managers can match people with jobs that play to their expertise and their skills in creative thinking, *and* ignite intrinsic motivation. Perfect matches stretch employees' abilities. The amount of stretch, however, is crucial: not so little that they feel bored but not so much that they feel overwhelmed and threatened by a loss of control.

Making a good match requires that managers possess rich and detailed information about their employees and the available assignments. Such information is often difficult and time consuming to gather. Perhaps that's why good matches are so rarely made. In fact, one of the most common ways managers kill creativity is by not trying to obtain the information necessary to make good connections between people and jobs. Instead, something of a shotgun wedding occurs. The most eligible employee is wed to the most eligible—that is, the most urgent and open—assignment. Often, the results are predictably unsatisfactory for all involved.

FREEDOM

When it comes to granting freedom, the key to creativity is giving people autonomy concerning the means—that is, concerning process—but not necessarily the ends. People will be more creative, in other words, if you give them freedom to decide how to climb a particular mountain. You needn't let them choose which mountain to climb. In fact, clearly specified strategic goals often enhance people's creativity.

I'm not making the case that managers should leave their subordinates entirely out of goal- or agenda-setting discussions. But they should understand that inclusion in those discussions will not necessarily enhance creative output and certainly will not be sufficient to do so. It is far more important that whoever sets the goals also makes them clear to the organization and that these goals remain stable for a meaningful period of time. It is difficult, if not impossible, to work creatively toward a target if it keeps moving.

Autonomy around process fosters creativity because giving people freedom in how they approach their work heightens their intrinsic motivation and sense of ownership. Freedom about process also allows people to approach problems in ways that make the most of their expertise and their creative-thinking skills. The task may end up being a stretch for them, but they can use their strengths to meet the challenge.

How do executives mismanage freedom? There are two common ways. First, managers tend to change goals frequently or fail to define them clearly. Employees may have freedom around process, but if they don't know where they are headed, such freedom is pointless. And second, some managers fall short on this dimension by granting autonomy in name only. They claim that employees are "empowered" to explore the maze as they search for solutions but, in fact, the process is proscribed. Employees diverge at their own risk.

RESOURCES

The two main resources that affect creativity are time and money. Managers need to allot these resources carefully. Like matching people with the right assignments, deciding how much time and money to give to a team or project is a sophisticated judgment call that can either support or kill creativity.

Consider time. Under some circumstances, time pressure can heighten creativity. Say, for instance, that a competitor is about to launch a great product at a lower price than your offering or that society faces a serious problem and desperately needs a solution—such as an AIDS vaccine. In such situations, both the time crunch and the importance of the work legitimately make people feel that they must rush. Indeed, cases like these would be apt to

Deciding how much time and money to give to a team or project is a judgment call that can either support or kill creativity.

increase intrinsic motivation by increasing the sense of
challenge.

Organizations routinely kill creativity with fake deadlines or impossibly tight ones. The former create distrust
and the latter cause burnout. In either case, people feel
overcontrolled and unfulfilled—which invariably damages motivation. Moreover, creativity often takes time. It
can be slow going to explore new concepts, put together
unique solutions, and wander through the maze. Managers who do not allow time for exploration or do not
schedule in incubation periods are unwittingly standing
in the way of the creative process.

When it comes to project resources, again managers
must make a fit. They must determine the funding,
people, and other resources that a team legitimately
needs to complete an assignment—and they must know
how much the organization can legitimately afford to
allocate to the assignment. Then they must strike a compromise. Interestingly, adding more resources above a
"threshold of sufficiency" does not boost creativity.
Below that threshold, however, a restriction of resources
can dampen creativity. Unfortunately, many managers
don't realize this and therefore often make another mistake. They keep resources tight, which pushes people to
channel their creativity into finding additional
resources, not in actually developing new products or
services.

Another resource that is misunderstood when it
comes to creativity is physical space. It is almost conventional wisdom that creative teams need open, comfortable offices. Such an atmosphere won't hurt creativity,
and it may even help, but it is not nearly as important as
other managerial initiatives that influence creativity.

Indeed, a problem we have seen time and time again is managers paying attention to creating the "right" physical space at the expense of more high-impact actions, such as matching people to the right assignments and granting freedom around work processes.

WORK-GROUP FEATURES

If you want to build teams that come up with creative ideas, you must pay careful attention to the design of such teams. That is, you must create mutually supportive groups with a diversity of perspectives and backgrounds. Why? Because when teams comprise people with various intellectual foundations and approaches to work—that is, different expertise and creative-thinking styles—ideas often combine and combust in exciting and useful ways.

Diversity, however, is only a starting point. Managers must also make sure that the teams they put together have three other features. First, the members must share excitement over the team's goal. Second, members must display a willingness to help their teammates through difficult periods and setbacks. And third, every member must recognize the unique knowledge and perspective that other members bring to the table. These factors enhance not only intrinsic motivation but also expertise and creative-thinking skills.

Again, creating such teams requires managers to have a deep understanding of their people. They must be able to assess them not just for their knowledge but for their attitudes about potential fellow team members and the collaborative process, for their problem-solving styles, and for their motivational hot buttons. Putting together a team with just the right chemistry—just the right level of diversity and supportiveness—can be difficult, but our research shows how powerful it can be.

It follows, then, that one common way managers kill creativity is by assembling homogeneous teams. The lure to do so is great. Homogeneous teams often reach "solutions" more quickly and with less friction along the way. These teams often report high morale, too. But homogeneous teams do little to enhance expertise and creative thinking. Everyone comes to the table with a similar mind-set. They leave with the same.

SUPERVISORY ENCOURAGEMENT

Most managers are extremely busy. They are under pressure for results. It is therefore easy for them to let praise for creative efforts—not just creative successes but unsuccessful efforts, too—fall by the wayside. One very simple step managers can take to foster creativity is to not let that happen.

The connection to intrinsic motivation here is clear. Certainly, people can find their work interesting or exciting without a cheering section—for some period of time. But to *sustain* such passion, most people need to feel as if their work matters to the organization or to some important group of people. Otherwise, they might as well do their work at home and for their own personal gain.

In many companies, new ideas are met not with open minds but with time-consuming layers of evaluation.

Managers in successful, creative organizations rarely offer specific extrinsic rewards for particular outcomes. However, they freely and generously recognize creative work by individuals and teams—often before the ultimate commercial impact of those efforts is known. By contrast, managers who kill creativity do so either by failing to acknowledge innovative efforts or by greeting them with skepticism. In many companies, for instance, new ideas are met not with open minds but with time-consuming layers of evaluation—or even with harsh criticism. When someone suggests a new product or process, senior managers take weeks to respond. Or they put that person through an excruciating critique.

Not every new idea is worthy of consideration, of course, but in many organizations, managers habitually demonstrate a reaction that damages creativity. They look for reasons to not use a new idea instead of searching for reasons to explore it further. An interesting psychological dynamic underlies this phenomenon. Our research shows that people believe that they will appear smarter to their bosses if they are more critical—and it often works. In many organizations, it is professionally rewarding to react critically to new ideas.

Unfortunately, this sort of negativity bias can have severe consequences for the creativity of those being evaluated. How? First, a culture of evaluation leads people to focus on the external rewards and punishments associated with their output, thus increasing the presence of extrinsic motivation and its potentially negative effects on intrinsic motivation. Second, such a culture creates a climate of fear, which again undermines intrinsic motivation.

Finally, negativity also shows up in how managers treat people whose ideas don't pan out: often, they are terminated or otherwise warehoused within the organization. Of course, ultimately, ideas do need to work; remember that creative ideas in business must be new *and* useful. The dilemma is that you can't possibly know beforehand which ideas will pan out. Furthermore, dead ends can sometimes be very enlightening. In many business situations, knowing what doesn't work can be as useful as knowing what does. But if people do not perceive any "failure value" for projects that ultimately do not achieve commercial success, they'll become less and less likely to experiment, explore, and connect with their work on a personal level. Their intrinsic motivation will evaporate.

Supervisory encouragement comes in other forms besides rewards and punishment. Another way managers can support creativity is to serve as role models, persevering through tough problems as well as encouraging collaboration and communication within the team. Such behavior enhances all three components of the creative process, and it has the added virtue of being a high-impact practice that a single manager can take on his or her own. It is better still when all managers in an organization serve as role models for the attitudes and behaviors that encourage and nurture creativity.

ORGANIZATIONAL SUPPORT

Encouragement from supervisors certainly fosters creativity, but creativity is truly enhanced when the entire organization supports it. Such support is the job of an organization's leaders, who must put in place appropriate systems or procedures and emphasize values that make it clear that creative efforts are a top priority. For example, creativity-supporting organizations consistently reward creativity, but they avoid using money to "bribe" people to come up with innovative ideas. Because monetary rewards make people feel as if they are being controlled, such a tactic probably won't work. At the same time, not providing sufficient recognition and rewards for creativity can spawn negative feelings within an organization. People can feel used, or at the least underappreciated, for their creative efforts. And it is rare to find the energy and passion of intrinsic motivation coupled with resentment.

Most important, an organization's leaders can support creativity by mandating information sharing and collaboration and by ensuring that political problems do not fester. Information sharing and collaboration support all three components of creativity. Take expertise. The more often people exchange ideas and data by working together, the more knowledge they will have. The same dynamic can be said for creative thinking. In fact, one way to enhance the creative thinking of employees is to expose them to various approaches to problem solving. With the exception of hardened misanthropes, information sharing and collaboration heighten peoples' enjoyment of work and thus their intrinsic motivation.

Whether or not you are seeking to enhance creativity, it is probably never a good idea to let political problems fester in an organizational setting. Infighting, politicking, and gossip are particularly damaging to creativity because they take peoples' attention away from work. That sense of mutual purpose and excitement so central to intrinsic motivation invariably lessens when people are cliquish or at war with one another. Indeed, our research suggests that intrinsic motivation increases when people are aware that those around them are excited by their jobs. When political problems abound, people feel that their work is threatened by others' agendas.

Finally, politicking also undermines expertise. The reason? Politics get in the way of open communication, obstructing the flow of information from point A to point B. Knowledge stays put and expertise suffers.

From the Individual to the Organization

Can executives build entire organizations that support creativity? The answer is yes. Consider the results of an intensive research project we recently completed called the Team Events Study. Over the course of two years, we studied more than two dozen teams in seven companies across three industries: high tech, consumer products, and chemicals. By following each team every day through the entire course of a creative project, we had a window into the details of what happened as the project progressed—or failed to progress, as the case may be. We did this through daily confidential e-mail reports from every person on each of the teams. At the end of each project, and at several points along the way, we used confidential reports from company experts and from team members to assess the level of creativity used in problem solving as well as the overall success of the project.

As might be expected, the teams and the companies varied widely in how successful they were at producing creative work. One organization, which I will call Chemical Central Research, seemed to be a veritable hotbed of creativity. Chemical Central supplied its parent organization with new formulations for a wide variety of industrial and consumer products. In many respects, however, members of Chemical Central's development teams were unremarkable. They were well educated, but no more so than people in many other companies we had studied. The company was doing well financially, but not enormously better than most other companies. What seemed to distinguish this organization was the quality of leadership at both the top-management level and the team level. The way managers formed teams, communicated with them, and supported their work enabled them to establish an organization in which creativity was continually stimulated.

We saw managers making excellent matches between people and assignments again and again at Chemical Central. On occasion, team members were initially unsure of whether they were up to the challenge they were given. Almost invariably, though, they found their passion and interest growing through a deep involvement in the work. Their managers knew to match them with jobs that had them working at the top of their competency levels, pushing the frontiers of their skills, and developing new competencies. But managers were careful not to allow too big a gap between employees' assignments and their abilities.

Moreover, managers at Chemical Central collaborated with the teams from the outset of a project to clarify goals. The final goals, however, were set by the managers. Then, at the day-to-day operational level, the teams were given a great deal of autonomy to make their own decisions about product development. Throughout the project, the teams' leaders and top-level managers periodically checked to see that work was directed toward the overall goals. But people were given real freedom around the implementation of the goals.

As for work-group design, every Chemical Central team, though relatively small (between four and nine members), included members of diverse professional and ethnic backgrounds. Occasionally, that diversity led to communication difficulties. But more often, it sparked new insights and allowed the teams to come up with a wider variety of ways to accomplish their goals.

One team, for example, was responsible for devising a new way to make a major ingredient for one of the company's most important products. Because managers at Chemical Central had worked consciously to create a diverse team, it happened that one member had both a legal and a technical background. This person realized that the team might well be able to patent its core idea, giving the company a clear advantage in a new market. Because team members were mutually supportive, that member was willing and eager to work closely with the inventor. Together, these individuals helped the team navigate its way through the patent application process. The team was successful and had fun along the way.

Supervisory encouragement and organizational support were also widespread at Chemical Central. For instance, a member of one team received a company award as an outstanding scientist even though, along the way, he had experienced many failures as well as successes. At one point, after spending a great deal of time on one experiment, he told us, "All I came up with was a pot of junk." Still, the company did not punish or warehouse him because of a creative effort that had failed. Instead, he was publicly lauded for his consistently creative work.

Finally, Chemical Central's leaders did much to encourage teams to seek support from all units within their divisions and to encourage collaboration across all quarters. The general manager of the research unit himself set an example, offering both strategic and technical ideas whenever teams approached him for help. Indeed, he explicitly made cross-team support a priority among top scientists in the organization. As a result, such support was expected and recognized.

For example, one team was about to test a new formulation for one of the company's major products. Because the team was small, it had to rely on a materials-analysis group within the organization to help conduct the tests. The analysis group not only helped out but also set aside generous blocks of time during the week before testing to help the team understand the nature and limits of the information the group would provide, when they would have it, and what they would need from the team to support them effectively. Members of the team were confident that they could rely on the materials-analysis group throughout the process, and the trials went well— despite the usual technical difficulties encountered in such testing.

By contrast, consider what we observed at another company in our study, a consumer-products company we'll call National Houseware Products. For years, National had been well known for its innovation. But recently, the company had been restructured to accommodate a major growth spurt, and many senior managers had been fired or transferred. National's work environment had undergone drastic changes. At the same time, new product successes and new business ideas seemed to be slowing to a trickle. Interestingly, the daily reports of the Team

Managers at one company undermined employees' creativity by continually changing goals and interfering with processes.

Events Study revealed that virtually all creativity killers were present.

Managers undermined autonomy by continually changing goals and interfering with processes. At one quarterly review meeting, for example, four priorities that had been defined by management at the previous quarterly review meeting were not even mentioned. In another instance, a product that had been identified as the team's number one project was suddenly dropped without explanation.

Resources were similarly mismanaged. For instance, management perennially put teams under severe and seemingly arbitrary time and resource constraints. At first, many team members were energized by the fire-fighting atmosphere. They threw themselves into their work and rallied. But after a few months, their verve had diminished, especially because the pressures had proved meaningless.

But perhaps National's managers damaged creativity most with their approach to evaluation. They were routinely critical of new suggestions. One employee told us that he was afraid to tell his managers about some radical ideas that he had developed to grow his area of the business. The employee was wildly enthusiastic about the potential for his ideas but ultimately didn't mention them to any of his bosses. He wondered why he should bother talking about new ideas when each one was studied for all its flaws instead of its potential. Through its actions, management had too often sent the message that any big ideas about how to change the status quo would be carefully scrutinized. Those individuals brave enough to suggest new ideas had to endure long—often nasty—meetings, replete with suspicious questions.

In another example, when a team took a new competitive pricing program to the boss, it was told that a discussion of the idea would have to wait another month. One exasperated team member noted, "We analyze so long, we've lost the business before we've taken any action at all!"

Yet another National team had put in particularly long hours over a period of several weeks to create a radically improved version of a major product. The team succeeded in bringing out the product on time and in budget, and it garnered promising market response. But management acted as if everything were business as usual, providing no recognition or reward to the team. A couple of months later, when we visited the team to report the results of our study, we learned that the team leader had just accepted a job from a smaller competitor. He confided that although he felt that the opportunities for advancement and ultimate visibility may have been greater at National, he believed his work and his ideas would be valued more highly somewhere else.

And finally, the managers at National allowed political problems to fester. Consider the time a National team came up with a great idea to save money in manufacturing a new product—which was especially urgent because a competitor had just come out with a similar product at a lower price. The plan was nixed. As a matter of "policy"—a code word for long-held allegiances and rivalries within the company—the manufacturing division wouldn't allow it. One team member commented, "If facts and figures instead of politics reigned supreme, this would be a no-brainer. There are no definable cost savings from running the products where they do, and there is no counterproposal on how to save the money another way. It's just 'No!' because this is the way they want it."

Great Rewards and Risks

The important lesson of the National and Chemical Central stories is that fostering creativity is in the hands of managers as they think about, design, and establish the work environment. Creativity often requires that managers radically change the ways in which they build and interact with work groups. In many respects, it calls for a conscious culture change. But it can be done, and the rewards can be great.

The risks of not doing so may be even greater. When creativity is killed, an organization loses a potent competitive weapon: new ideas. It can also lose the energy and commitment of its people. Indeed, in all my years of research into creativity, perhaps the most difficult part has been hearing people complain that they feel stifled, frustrated, and shut down by their organizations. As one team member at National told us, "By the time I get home every day, I feel physically, emotionally, and intellectually drained. Help!"

Fostering creativity often requires that managers radically change how they build and interact with work groups.

Even if organizations seemed trapped in organizational ecosystems that kill creativity—as in the case of National Houseware Products—it is still possible to effect widespread change. Consider a recent transformation at Procter & Gamble. Once a hotbed of creativity, P&G had in recent years seen the number of its product innovations decline significantly. In response, the company established Corporate New Ventures (CNV), a small cross-functional team that embodies many of the creativity-enhancing practices described in this article.

In terms of challenge, for instance, members of the CNV team were allowed to elect themselves. How better to make sure someone is intrinsically motivated for an assignment than to ask for volunteers? Building a team from volunteers, it should be noted, was a major departure from standard P&G procedures. Members of the CNV team also were given a clear, challenging strategic goal: to invent radical new products that would build the company's future. Again departing from typical P&G practices, the team was given enormous latitude around how, when, and where they approached their work.

The list of how CNV broke with P&G's creativity-killing practices is a long one. On nearly every creativity-support dimension in the KEYS work-environment survey, CNV scored higher than national norms and higher than the pre-CNV environment at P&G. But more important than the particulars is the question: Has the changed environment resulted in more creative work? Undeniably so, and the evidence is convincing. In the three years since its inception, CNV has handed off 11 projects to the business sectors for execution. And as of early 1998, those products were beginning to flow out of the pipeline. The first product, designed to provide portable heat for several hours' relief of minor pain, was already in test marketing. And six other products were slated to go to test market within a year. Not surprisingly, given CNV's success, P&G is beginning to expand both the size and the scope of its CNV venture.

Even if you believe that your organization fosters creativity, take a hard look for creativity killers. Some of

them may be flourishing in a dark corner—or even in
the light. But rooting out creativity-killing behaviors
isn't enough. You have to make a conscious effort to
support creativity. The result can be a truly innovative
company where creativity doesn't just survive but actually thrives.

The Creativity Maze

TO UNDERSTAND THE differences between extrinsic
and intrinsic motivation, imagine a business problem as
a maze.

One person might be motivated to make it through
the maze as quickly and safely as possible in order to
get a tangible reward, such as money—the same way a
mouse would rush through for a piece of cheese. This
person would look for the simplest, most straightforward
path and then take it. In fact, if he is in a real rush to
get that reward, he might just take the most beaten
path and solve the problem exactly as it has been
solved before.

That approach, based on extrinsic motivation, will
indeed get him out of the maze. But the solution that
arises from the process is likely to be unimaginative. It
won't provide new insights about the nature of the problem or reveal new ways of looking at it. The rote solution
probably won't move the business forward.

Another person might have a different approach to the
maze. She might actually find the process of wandering
around the different paths—the challenge and exploration
itself—fun and intriguing. No doubt, this journey will take

longer and include mistakes, because any maze—any truly complex problem—has many more dead ends than exits. But when the intrinsically motivated person finally does find a way out of the maze—a solution—it very likely will be more interesting than the rote algorithm. It will be more creative.

There is abundant evidence of strong intrinsic motivation in the stories of widely recognized creative people. When asked what makes the difference between creative scientists and those who are less creative, the Nobel-prize-winning physicist Arthur Schawlow said, "The labor-of-love aspect is important. The most successful scientists often are not the most talented, but the ones who are just impelled by curiosity. They've got to know what the answer is." Albert Einstein talked about intrinsic motivation as "the enjoyment of seeing and searching." The novelist John Irving, in discussing the very long hours he put into his writing, said, "The unspoken factor is love. The reason I can work so hard at my writing is that it's not work for me." And Michael Jordan, perhaps the most creative basketball player ever, had a "love of the game" clause inserted into his contract; he insisted that he be free to play pick-up basketball games any time he wished.

Creative people are rarely superstars like Michael Jordan. Indeed, most of the creative work done in the business world today gets done by people whose names will never be recorded in history books. They are people with expertise, good creative-thinking skills, and high levels of intrinsic motivation. And just as important, they work in organizations where managers consciously build environments that support these characteristics instead of destroying them.

Suggested Readings

Teresa M. Amabile, *Creativity in Context: Update to the Social Psychology of Creativity* (Boulder, Colo.: Westview Press, 1996).

Teresa M. Amabile, Robert Burnside, and Stanley S. Gryskiewicz, *User's Manual for KEYS: Assessing the Climate for Creativity* (Greensboro, N.C.: Center for Creative Leadership, 1998).

Rosabeth Moss Kanter, *Frontiers of Management* (Boston, Mass.: Harvard Business School Press, 1997).

Originally published in September–October 1998
Reprint 98501

Spark Innovation through Empathic Design

DOROTHY LEONARD AND

JEFFREY F. RAYPORT

Executive Summary

COMPANIES ARE USED TO BRINGING in customers to participate in focus groups, usability laboratories, and market research surveys in order to help in the development of new products and services. And for improving products that customers know well, those tools are highly sophisticated. For example, knowledgeable customers are adept at identifying the specific scent of leather they expect in a luxury vehicle or at helping to tune the sound of a motorcycle engine to just the timbre that evokes feelings of power.

But to go beyond the improvements to the familiar, companies need to identify and meet needs that customers may not yet recognize. To accomplish that task, a set of techniques called empathic design can help.

Rather than bring the customers to the company, empathic design calls for company representatives to

29

watch customers using products and services in the context of their own environments. By doing so, managers can often identify unexpected uses for their products, just as the product manager of cooking oil did when he observed a neighbor spraying the oil on the blades of a lawn mower to reduce grass buildup. They can also uncover problems that customers don't mention in surveys, as the president of Nissan Design did when he watched a couple struggling to remove the backseat of a competitor's minivan in order to transport a couch.

The five-step process Dorothy Leonard and Jeffrey Rayport describe in detail is a relatively low-cost, low-risk way to identify customer needs, and it has the potential to redirect a companies' existing technological capabilities toward entirely new businesses.

ALMOST EVERY COMPANY COMPETES to some degree on the basis of continual innovation. And to be commercially successful, new product and service ideas must, of course, meet a real—or perceived—customer need. Hence the current managerial mantras: "Get close to the customer" and "Listen to the voice of the customer." The problem is, customers' ability to guide the development of new products and services is limited by their experience and their ability to imagine and describe possible innovations. How can companies identify needs that customers themselves may not recognize? How can designers develop ways to meet those needs, if even in the course of extensive market research, customers never mention their desires because they assume those desires can't be fulfilled?

A set of techniques we call *empathic design* can help resolve those dilemmas. At its foundation is observation—watching consumers use products or services. But unlike in focus groups, usability laboratories, and other contexts of traditional market research, such observation is conducted in the customer's own environment—in the course of normal, everyday routines. In such a context, researchers can gain access to a host of information that is not accessible through other observation-oriented research methods.

The techniques of empathic design—gathering, analyzing, and applying information gleaned from observation in the field—are familiar to top engineering/design companies and to a few forward-thinking manufacturers, but they are not common practice. Nor are they taught in marketing courses, being more akin to anthropology than marketing science. In fact, few companies are set up to employ empathic design; the techniques require unusual collaborative skills that many organizations have not developed. Market researchers generally use text or numbers to spark ideas for new products, but empathic designers use visual information as well. Traditional researchers are generally trained to gather data in relative isolation from other disciplines; empathic design demands creative interactions among members of an interdisciplinary team.

Developing the expertise, however, is a worthy investment. Empathic design is a relatively low-cost, low-risk way to identify potentially critical customer needs. It's an important source of new product ideas, and it has the potential to redirect a company's technological capabilities toward entirely new businesses.

When Questions Don't Yield Answers

When a product or service is well understood, traditional marketing science provides amazingly sophisticated

ways to gain useful information from potential customers and influence their purchasing decisions. Consider how subtle are preferences of smell and sound, yet
car manufacturers can design automobile interiors to
evoke the specific scent of expensive leather that U.S.
buyers expect in a luxury vehicle. Nissan Design International tested more than 90 samples of leather before
selecting 3 that U.S.
noses preferred for the
Infinity J-30. Similarly,
manufacturers are adept
at fine-tuning engines so
that they make the pre-
ferred sounds associated

*Sometimes, customers are
so accustomed to
current conditions that
they don't think to
ask for a new solution.*

with surging power and swift acceleration. Harley-
Davidson, in fact, has sued competitors that have imi-
tated the voices of its motors, which have been carefully
adjusted to please its customers' ears. Customers can
guide an auto or motorcycle manufacturer in making
even minute adjustments in its offering because they are
familiar with the products and have developed over
time a finely honed set of desires and perceived needs. In
fact, the driving experience is so deeply ingrained that
they can re-create most of the needs they encounter
while on the road even when they are not actually in the
driver's seat.

The practices of traditional marketing science are
also effective in situations where consumers are already
familiar with a proposed solution to a problem because
of their experiences with it in a different context. Peel-
away postage stamps were an innovation that customers
could comprehend because they had already encountered the light adhesives used in Post-it Notes and peel-
away labels.

But sometimes, customers are so accustomed to current conditions that they don't think to ask for a new solution—even if they have real needs that could be addressed. Habit tends to inure us to inconvenience; as consumers, we create "work-arounds" that become so familiar we may forget that we are being forced to behave in a less-than-optimal fashion—and thus we may be incapable of telling market researchers what we really want.

For example, when asked about an editing function in a software package, one customer had no complaints— until she sat down to use the program in front of the observer. Then she realized that her work was disrupted when the program did not automatically wrap text around graphics while she edited. Accustomed to working around the problem, she had not mentioned it in earlier interviews.

Market research is generally unhelpful when a company has developed a new technological capability that is not tied to a familiar consumer paradigm. If no current product exists in the market that embodies at least the most primitive form of a new product, consumers have no foundation on which to formulate their opinions. When radio technology was first introduced in the early twentieth century, it was used solely for transmitting Morse code and voice communication from point to point. Only after David Sarnoff suggested in 1915 that such technology could be better employed in broadcasting news, music, and baseball games was the "radio music box" born. Sarnoff had put his knowledge of the technology together with what he found when he observed families gathered in their homes to envision a totally different use for the technology. No one had asked for broadcasting because they didn't know it was feasible.

So there are many reasons why standard techniques of inquiry rarely lead to truly novel product concepts. It is extremely difficult to design an instrument for market research that is amenable to quantitative analysis and also open-ended enough to capture a customer's environment completely. Market researchers have to contend with respondents' tendency to try to please the inquirer by providing expected answers, as well as their inclination to avoid embarrassment by not revealing practices they suspect might be deemed inappropriate. The people who design surveys, run focus groups, and interview customers further cloud the results by inadvertently—and inevitably—introducing their own biases into the questioning. When a customer's needs are solicited in writing or through constrained dialogue, pummeled with statistical logic, and delivered to product developers in compressed form, critical information may be missing. But why would observation be a better approach?

What We Learn from Observation

Watching consumers has always yielded obvious, but still tremendously valuable, basic information. Consider usability: Is the package difficult to open? Does the user have to resort to the manual, or are operating principles clearly telegraphed by the design? Are handles, knobs, and distances from the floor designed ergonomically? Does the user hesitate or seem confused at any point? What unspoken and possibly false assumptions are guiding the user's interaction with the product?

You can easily get that sort of feedback by watching people work with your products in usability labs and by testing for various ergonomic requirements. It is the additional information gained from seeing your customers actually use your product or service in their own physical environment that makes empathic design an imperative. Empathic-design techniques can yield at least five types of information that cannot be gathered through traditional marketing or product research.

Triggers of use. What circumstances prompt people to use your product or service? Do your customers turn to your offering when, and in the way, you expected? If they don't, there may be an opportunity for your company.

Consider what Hewlett-Packard learned in the early 1990s by observing users of the HP 95/100 LX series of personal digital assistants (PDAs). The company allied itself with Lotus Development Corporation to produce the PDA mainly because its product developers knew that their "road warrior" consumers valued the computing power of Lotus 1-2-3 spreadsheet software. But when HP's researchers watched customers actually using the product, they found that the personal-organizer software the company had also licensed from Lotus was at least as important a trigger for using the PDA as the spreadsheet was.

When the makers of Cheerios went out in the field, they found that breakfast wasn't necessarily the primary purpose for which certain households were using the cereal. Parents of small children, they found, were more interested in the fact that the pieces could be bagged, carried, and doled out one by one as a tidy snack anytime, anywhere to occupy restless tots.

And when the brand manager for a spray-on cooking oil saw his neighbor using the product on the bottom of his lawn mower, he discovered an entirely unexpected trigger. Pressed to explain, the neighbor pointed out that the oil prevented cut grass from adhering to the bottom of the mower and did no harm to the lawn. Such unanticipated usage patterns can identify opportunities not only for innovation and product redesign but also for entering entirely new markets.

Interactions with the user's environment. How does your product or service fit into your users' own idiosyncratic systems—whether they be a household routine, an office operation, or a manufacturing process? Consider what Intuit, maker of the personal-finance software package Quicken, learns through its "Follow Me Home" program, in which product developers gain permission from first-time buyers to observe their initial experience with the software in their own homes. Intuit, of course, learns a good deal about its product's packaging, documentation, and installation from this exercise, as well as about the user friendliness of its software. But it can gather that kind of information in a usability laboratory. What Intuit can't reliably learn in any way other than by watching someone boot up Quicken on a home computer is what other software applications are running on that customer's system and how that software can interfere with or complement Quicken's own operation. Moreover, product developers can see what other data files the customer refers to and might wish to access directly, what state of organization or disarray such files are in, and whether they are on paper or in electronic form. It was from such in-home observations that Intuit designers discovered that many small-business owners were using Quicken to keep their books.

Some small changes that can result from watching people use your product in their own environment can also be competitively important. When engineers from a manufacturer of laboratory equipment visited a customer, they noticed that the equipment emitted a high level of air pollution when it was being used for certain applications. That observation motivated the company to add a venting hood to its product line. Current users were so accustomed to the unpleasant smell that they had never thought to mention it and didn't regard a venting hood as an important enhancement—until it was available. Then the company's sales force found the hood to be a compelling sales point when customers compared the product with those of competitors.

User customization. Do users reinvent or redesign your product to serve their own purposes? Producers of industrial equipment observed users taping pieces of paper to their product to serve as identifying labels. The manufacturer gained an inexpensive, but appreciable, advantage over the competition when it incorporated a flat protected space for such machine-specific information into its next model. And every Japanese automaker has set up a design studio in southern California because fanatical car owners there are prone to modifying their cars, often substantially, to meet their particular desires, be they functional (more cargo space, larger engines) or ego-intensive (spoilers, special wheels, new colors). Observing these users helps designers at Nissan and Toyota envision the potential evolution of specific models— and gives them a window on the possible future of cars and trucks in general.

Sometimes, users combine several existing products to solve a problem, not only revealing new uses for traditional products but also highlighting their shortcomings. A prominent producer of household cleaners handed video cameras to family members to record how its products were really being used in people's basements. The company then could see homemakers concocting their own recipes for particular household chores, such as washing white curtains ("one cup baking soda, one cup dishwashing detergent," and so on).

Similarly, in the course of studying consumers' mobile-communication needs, consultants at the Chicago-based Doblin Group, observed individuals creatively combining beepers and cell phones so they could be just as available as they wished—and no more. These consumers gave special beeper codes to friends and relatives to screen out undesired interruptions. That suggested to the firm the need for filtering capabilities on cell phones.

Observers saw people combining beepers and cell phones not to answer calls but to screen them.

Intangible attributes of the product. What kinds of peripheral or intangible attributes does your product or service have? Customers rarely name such attributes in focus groups or surveys, but those unseen factors may constitute a kind of emotional franchise—and thus an opportunity. When watching videos of homemakers using cleansers and detergents, representatives of the household-products company could see how often the smell of the products evoked satisfaction with their use, engendered feelings of nostalgia ("My mother used this") or elicited other emotional responses ("When it smells clean, it makes all my work worthwhile").

Such intangible, invisible product assets can be augmented, exploited, or redirected. After visiting the homes of Kimberly-Clark customers, consultants at the Palo Alto, California-based design firm GVO recognized the emotional appeal of pull-on diapers to parents and toddlers, who saw them as a step toward "grown-up" dress. Diapers were clothing, the observers realized, and had highly symbolic as well as functional meaning. Huggies Pull-Ups were rolled out nationally in 1991, and by the time competitors caught on, the company was selling $400 million worth of the product annually.

Failing to note such intangible attributes can sink a new product. Environmentally friendly disks that clean washer loads of clothes without detergents have yet to attract a mass market—in large part, according to the Doblin Group's observational research, because they don't produce the expected clean-clothes smell.

Unarticulated user needs. The application of empathic design that holds the greatest potential benefit is the observation of current or possible customers encountering problems with your products or services that they don't know can be addressed and may not even recognize as problems. What do you see people being unable to do that would clearly be beneficial?

A product developer from Hewlett-Packard sat in an operating room observing a surgeon at work. The surgeon was guiding his scalpel by watching the patient's body and his own hands displayed on a television screen. As nurses walked around the room, they would periodically obscure the surgeon's view of the screen and the operation for a few seconds. No one complained. But this unacknowledged problem caused the developer to ponder the possibility of creating a lightweight helmet that could suspend the images a few inches in front of the surgeon's eyes. Her company had the technology to create such a product. The surgeon would never have thought to ask for it, even though its potential to improve productivity, increase accuracy, and make the surgeon's work easier was substantial.

Unarticulated needs abound in daily routines, even when a technological solution exists. For example, Nissan Design's president, Jerry Hirshberg, was driving along a freeway one day when he saw a couple at the side of the road wrestling the back seat of a competitor's minivan out of the way so they could pick up a new couch. "We bought this so we would have room," they told him, "but we can't use it for what we want without taking out the seats." They would never have thought of asking for any solution to their problem, but one immediately occurred to Hirshberg—six-foot runners that would enable van owners to fold up the backseats and slide them out of the way, thus easily creating cargo room.

Weyerhaeuser won an important advantage in the market for particle board after observing an unarticulated need during a visit to a customer's plant. The customer, a major furniture maker, created table legs by laminating together narrow boards produced by some of Weyerhaeuser's competitors. Unable either to match the competitors' prices or to convince the customer to pay higher prices for superior quality, Weyerhaeuser instead came up with a new way to make table legs—a new, much thicker particle board that did not have to be laminated. The consequent savings to customers in tooling and labor costs put Weyerhaeuser back in the competitive running.

Some stunning product ideas come from an engineer or designer who actually uses the products he or she develops because this individual combines knowledge of unexpressed needs with knowledge of how to fill those needs. U.S. women were annoyed for years by the inappropriateness of using a man's safety razor, designed for faces, on their underarms and legs. When a female designer reshaped the razor for a woman's hand and needs—the Gillette Lady Sensor—it was enormously successful.

The oft-repeated advice to "delight the customer" assumes real meaning when product or service providers push beyond what their customers anticipate to deliver the unexpected—and technology is a primary agent of such delight. But all companies have capabilities they are failing to tap in their quest to create innovative products and services because those who know what *can* be done are not generally in direct contact with those who *need* something done. Empathic-design techniques thus exploit a company's existing technological capabilities in the widest sense of the term. When a company's representatives explore their customers' worlds with the eyes of a fresh observer while simultaneously carrying the knowledge of what is possible for the company to do, they can redirect existing organizational capabilities toward new markets. Consider it a process of mining knowledge assets for new veins of innovation. Usually, much of the basic underlying technology or service methodologies already exist; they just need to be applied differently.

Empathic-design techniques can't replace market research; rather, they contribute to the flow of ideas that need further testing.

One important note: empathic-design techniques cannot replace market research; rather, they contribute to the flow of ideas that need further scientific testing before a company commits itself to any full-fledged development project.

Empathic Design: the Process

Companies can engage in empathic design, or similar techniques such as contextual inquiry, in a variety of ways. However, most employ the following five-step process.

STEP ONE: OBSERVATION

It's important to clarify who should be observed, who should do the observing, and what the observer should be watching.

Who should be observed? These individuals may be customers, noncustomers, the customers of customers, or a group of individuals who by playing different roles collectively perform a task.

Hewlett-Packard makes protocol analyzer software that enables managers of computer operations to diagnose network malfunctions. As networks became more complex, smaller companies began to offer customized software for the idiosyncratic needs of some of HP's customers. In response, HP designers conducted extensive market research, which resulted in a cacophony of requests to expand the types of data the analyzers could track and report on. Not only did that make product development much more difficult, it also failed to make the products any more effective. Users became inundated with data that they couldn't turn into useful information. HP developers decided to stop focusing on their traditional customers, the operations managers. Instead, they watched, among others, network maintenance technicians at work.

From those observations, the developers discovered that what their customers really needed was not, as they had been told, more data to analyze. Rather, users needed to recover swiftly from computer crashes. That change in perspective led to a shift in technological emphasis. The result was HP's highly successful Network Advisor, which de-emphasizes data collection, analysis, and reports. Instead, it identifies the network problem, recommends a solution, and suggests ways to implement the solution quickly. (See "Observing in Cyberspace" at the end of this article.)

Who should do the observing? Differences in training, education, and natural inclinations predispose different people to extract very different information when watching the exact same situation. A human-factors specialist may note body positions; an engineer may notice angles and mechanical interactions; a designer may see spaces and forms. Of course, many people are multiskilled observers, but the best way to capture the most important aspects of an environment is to send out a small team, each member of which has expertise in a different discipline. That's what the design firm IDEO did for Details, a subsidiary of the office-equipment supplier, Steelcase. To help Details develop a more easily repositioned computer keyboard, IDEO sent a human-factors expert, an engineer, and a designer on anthropological expeditions into office buildings. Each team member brought back a notebook full of very different data.

Because a critical objective of such an expedition is to match the unarticulated needs of users with technological possibilities, at least one member of any team should have experience in behavioral observation and another should have a deep understanding of the organizational capabilities the development team can draw upon. When the team comes from an outside consulting firm, some of the client's employees should be included to provide that deep understanding. The Doblin Group, for example, was challenged to redefine the travel experience for SAS. It convened a very large team that included not only social scientists and information designers but also pilots and flight attendants from the airline. The airline employees understood SAS's capabilities in depth and also knew how proposed service innovations might require changes not just in operations but also in corporate culture.

Few organizations have large numbers of employees capable of conducting such anthropological expeditions. When asked what characteristics members of empathic-design teams should have, managers that employ those techniques list ones rarely found on most résumés: open-mindedness, observational skills, and curiosity. Human resource departments are not set up to screen for such abilities. Some companies, such as Intel and Xerox, have hired cultural anthropologists and social psychologists for their research, marketing, or product development departments because they are trained observers who have demonstrated an interest in human behavior. Other organizations outsource this kind of work to design firms, knowing that there are employees in such specialty companies with a variety of skills: experts in human factors, in graphics and visual design, and in engineering.

What behavior should be observed? The people being observed should be carrying out normal routines—playing, eating, relaxing, or working at home or at the office. For its research on mobile communications, the Doblin Group followed a lawyer from the moment she left her children at their day care center in the morning until after the children were in bed that night, revealing a wealth of communication needs that are often overlooked. Few people, of course, are totally oblivious to a team of people hanging over their shoulders, observing them at work or play. But a real-life atmosphere—even a slightly stilted one—is still better than the highly artificial setting of a focus-group conference room or a laboratory. For some products and services, team members may conduct their observations in a highly unobtrusive way simply by planting themselves in a public setting where people are going about their normal routines and watching behaviors more systematically than the usual sidewalk observer generally does.

STEP TWO: CAPTURING DATA

Because empathic-design techniques stress observation over inquiry, relatively few data are gathered through responses to questions. (See the table "Inquiry versus Observation: What's Different?") When they wish to know how to interpret people's actions, observers may ask a few very open-ended questions, such as "Why are you doing that?" They often carry a list of questions to prompt their own

Nissan designers were startled to see how many people were eating in trucks—"not just drinks, but whole spaghetti dinners!"

observations—for example, "What problems is the user encountering?" But most data are gathered from visual, auditory, and sensory cues. Thus empathic-design teams very frequently use photography and videography as tools.

Video can capture subtle, fleeting body language that may convey large amounts of information and store it for future review and analysis. For more than a decade, researchers at Xerox PARC, the Xerox Palo Alto Research Center, have videotaped users when they were confronted with a product such as a new copier machine. The researchers can see puzzled looks on the subjects' faces, they watch as people search for controls, and they can observe the kinds of automatic responses that happen when someone expects a control to be here or there and it is not. Such cues come and go within the span of mere seconds and are hard to capture in notes.

Even still photographs convey information that can be lost in verbal descriptions. Nissan Design International commissioned a photographer to travel to several cities and take pictures of people in trucks to better understand how they were being used as commuter and family cars. NDI designers were startled to discover how little their trucks (and those of competitors) were actually being used for the purposes being advertised and reported in market surveys. NDI president Hirshberg was surprised to see how many people were eating in trucks, recalling "not just drinks, but whole spaghetti dinners!" The designers also noticed how much people resembled their vehicles and how scuffed up some of the vehicles were. They began to

Photographs show spatial arrangements and details that may go unnoticed in the field.

wonder if some vehicles should be more like denim and look better the more worn they got.

Photographs or drawings (which artists and designers can produce on the spot) show spatial arrangements and contain details that may have gone unnoticed while the team was on location. When members of one

---

Inquiry versus Observation: What's Different?

Inquiry

1. People can't ask for what they don't know is technically possible.

2. People are generally highly unreliable reporters of their own behavior.

3. People tend to give answers they think are expected or desired.

4. People are less likely to recall their feelings about intangible characteristics of products and services when they aren't in the process of using them.

5. People's imaginations—and hence their desires—are bounded by their experience; they accept inadequacies and deficiencies in their environment as normal.

6. Questions are often biased and reflect inquirers' unrecognized assumptions.

7. Questioning interrupts the usual flow of people's natural activity.

8. Questioning stifles opportunities for users to suggest innovations.

Observation

1. Well-chosen observers have deep knowledge of corporate capabilities, including the extent of the company's technical expertise.

2. Observers rely on real actions rather than reported behavior.

3. People are not asked to respond to verbal stimuli; they give nonverbal cues of their feelings and responses through body language, in addition to spontaneous, unsolicited comments.

4. Using the actual product or a prototype, or engaging in the actual activity for which an innovation is being designed, stimulates comments about such intangibles as smells or emotions associated with the product's use.

5. Trained, technically sophisticated observers can see solutions to unarticulated needs.

6. Observation is open ended and varied; trained observers tend to cancel out one another's observational biases.

7. Observation, while almost never totally unobtrusive, interrupts normal activities less than questioning does.

8. Observers in the field often identify user innovations that can be duplicated and improved for the rest of the market.

observation team displayed on a bulletin board all the candid photos they took of the people they observed in an office building, they were struck by the snake pit of wires in which everyone's feet were stuck. That led their company to build in conduits for those wires in its next generation of dividers for modular offices. And pictures of backyard barbecues taken for the developers from the Thermos company who were working on a new charcoal grill showed women struggling with equipment designed for the generally greater height and upper body strength of men, who were (incorrectly) assumed to be the most likely outdoor family chefs.

STEP THREE: REFLECTION AND ANALYSIS

After gathering data in many forms, the team members return to reflect on what they have observed and to review their visual data with other colleagues. Those individuals—unhampered by possibly extraneous information, such as the reputations of the individuals or companies visited or the weather at the observation site—will focus on the data before them, and they, too, will see different things. They will ask questions that the team members may or may not be able to answer and that may well send them out for further observation. It is at this point that the team tries to identify all of its customers' possible problems and needs.

The IDEO team redesigning Lifeline Systems' personal-response unit for elderly people uncovered a potentially dangerous problem only after they shared their field data with colleagues. On leaving for an extended period, many users turned off their units so that Lifeline's monitoring staff would not mistake silence for an emergency. However, because the unit lacked an obvious status indicator, users often forgot to reactivate the units when they returned. The opportunity to improve the design was recognized by engineers who were not part of the original group of IDEO observers. Consequently, IDEO redesigned the product so that it indicated even to the vision impaired when it was turned off and automatically restarted when users tried to send their habitual "all is well" signals to the monitoring service.

STEP FOUR: BRAINSTORMING FOR SOLUTIONS

Brainstorming is a valuable part of any innovation process; within the empathic-design process, it is used specifically to transform the observations into graphic, visual representations of possible solutions. Design firms maintain that this step is often undervalued: "Our clients sometimes don't understand why brainstorming is expensive—and immensely productive—until they have sat in on a session. Then they usually go away shaking their heads, saying, 'Wow—that was really amazing!'" Although brainstorming is generally associated with a creative process, it is not undisciplined. Managers at IDEO tell their employees to heed five rules: defer judgment, build on the ideas of others, hold one conversation at a time, stay focused on the topic, and encourage wild ideas.

Such sessions are valuable not only for the ideas that pop up during the actual brainstorming session but also for the concepts and solutions that occur to people later, at home, because the seeds to them had been planted in their minds.

Companies that routinely hold brainstorming sessions as part of the empathic-design process need supporting infrastructure. That can be as low tech as a table covered in thick paper used for doodling and taking notes; when a session is over, team members can tear off the best ideas and take them home. It can be as high tech as the Idea Factory, a physical and virtual space being set up in San Francisco to help companies create next-generation products and business strategies. To facilitate collaborative work, the Idea Factory will boast workstations; customized groupware; and the latest white-board recording equipment, which can produce hard copies of whatever is written down or drawn on the board's surface.

STEP FIVE: DEVELOPING PROTOTYPES OF POSSIBLE SOLUTIONS

Clearly, prototypes are not unique to empathic design. But the more radical an innovation, of course, the harder it is to understand how it should look, function, and be used. Just as researchers gather useful visual data, so too can they stimulate communication by creating some physical representation of a new concept for a product or service. Prototypes are a critical part of the empathic-design process for at least three reasons:

- Prototypes clarify the concept of the new product or service for the development team.

- They enable the team to place its concept in front of other individuals who work in functions not formally represented on the team.

- They can stimulate reaction and foster discussion with potential customers of the innovation because of their concreteness.

Sometimes, two prototypes are used, one that emulates the function but not the form, and another that illustrates the ideal physical appearance of the intended product but doesn't work. In designing the outdoor grill, Thermos's Lifestyle team produced two models, which they called the Monitor and the Merrimack (after the Civil War ships). The Monitor was a functioning prototype, but the team considered it ugly; the Merrimack was sleek and stylish but was actually an inert object made of plastic foam. The company used both models to elicit feedback from consumers and retailers.

Simulations are also useful prototypes. And they need not be as computer-intensive and elaborate as the University of Illinois's CAVE, which simulates the three-dimensional space of a room and can be programmed to represent different environments, such as a factory. In fact, many useful simulations are not computerized at all. When Chaparral Steel Company wanted to design metal splash guards to put along the path of the white-hot metal bars that were moving toward the rolling mill, they positioned waterlogged plywood at various angles and heights to simulate different designs. The plywood was rapidly consumed by the hot metal, but not before the experimenters could learn what design worked best.

Role-playing is also a form of simulation. At Interval Research Corporation of Palo Alto, California, young twenty-something media-interface designers were outfitted with fogged glasses, gloves, and weights on their arms and legs so they could feel what it would be like for the very elderly to work prototype physical controls or use hand gestures in the air as a way to control the next generation of TVs, VCRs, and other electronic equipment. That simulation allowed the young researchers to apply their intensive knowledge of media possibilities within constraints that they could not otherwise personally experience (at least for some years).

Empathic Design as a Culture Shift

A common criticism of the kinds of innovative ideas arising through empathic design is, "But users haven't asked for that." Precisely. By the time they do, your competitors will have the same new-product ideas you have—and you will be in the "me-too" game of copying and improving their ideas. Empathic-design techniques involve a twist on the idea that new-product development should be guided by users. In this approach, they still do—they just don't know it.

Empathic design pushes innovation beyond producing the same thing only better. So for example, computer company managers who have been exposed to a deep cultural understanding of mobility no longer think only of making lighter, faster, and more durable laptops. Instead, they are challenged to consider other communication needs a portable computer might meet. Developing a deep, empathic understanding of users' unarticulated needs can challenge industry assumptions and lead to a shift in corporate strategy.

Observing in Cyberspace

THE TECHNIQUES OF empathic design are a natural for the physical marketplace: watching customers use a product or service in their own homes or offices provides a wealth of information about possible innovations in real time and with little or no distortion. But empathic design also has great potential in the virtual world, or the "marketspace." Increasingly, people conduct business transactions—from banking and investing to purchasing and installing software packages—through cyberspace. Observing behavior in that virtual realm can yield many of the same benefits as observation in the physical world. In fact, in many situations, the virtual form of empathic design can result in speedier, more targeted innovation because companies can "watch" many more people at any given time in cyberspace and spot needs and trends at the very instant they emerge.

For example, software developers are increasingly taking advantage of "plug-ins"—small modules of computer code that they can download directly from the Web through their Internet browsers and combine together to make larger applications. Microsoft and Netscape are highly interested in which plug-ins their customers are downloading via their respective browsers, Internet Explorer or Netscape Navigator. Both companies can directly observe users running the plug-ins, gaining clues about emerging customer needs. For example, many browser users have recently begun to experiment with Internet telephony—that is, they have begun to use software from companies such as VocalTec Communications to make long-distance phone calls for free over the Web. Responding to this trend, Microsoft and Netscape now offer browsers with Internet telephony built in.

Similarly, software designers, who often conduct beta tests of new products on the Web with large groups of "techies," have access to enormously varied virtual discussions about their products. Every time a company releases a beta version of software on the Web and invites hackers to find bugs, identify flaws, and suggest improvements, that company can harvest insights into future needs by observing how users customize and critique their products.

And the success of America Online can be attributed in part to the fact that its managers understood and acted on what they found when they observed customers' usage patterns. Originally, managers had believed that information services would drive their business, but they found that those offerings were not what users valued most. Rather, users valued the ability to communicate through virtual channels with one another. So AOL invested aggressively in creating venues for social interaction, ranging from chat rooms and E-mail to buddy lists and event forums.

When AOL has ignored the wisdom of observing and listening to its markets, it has stumbled badly. Witness the recent consumer backlash that occurred when the commercial on-line service announced that it would sell the phone numbers of its 8.5 million users to telemarketers for a hefty sum. It pays to stay close to users through physical or digital observation as they use or experience the product or service.

Of course, the techniques of empathic design do not translate directly from the physical world to the virtual one. In fact, some would argue that "observation" in the marketspace is simply capturing data. And to an extent it is, since all observation ultimately becomes a source of data about users. But data represent behavior. And therein lies much untapped potential—untapped because the techniques of empathic design demand a much more intensive approach to those data than most companies currently take. Empathic design requires researchers to think about a body of data as a window into consumers' behavior and then to use that information as the basis for innovation. That requires a substantial investment in reflection and analysis—something many companies have not yet made.

Companies observing in cyberspace also face the issue of where to draw the line when it comes to privacy. Observation in the marketspace is by nature unobtrusive and can be perceived as invasive. Customers do not want to be spied on. It is important to consider what customers may consider an invasion of privacy and when the customer should be allowed to set the boundaries on a company's observations. The Microsoft Network software originally scanned and reported back to Microsoft the other programs its users had on their hard drives. The purpose of the observation ostensibly was to help Microsoft make its products compatible with other vendors' software. But customers raised concerns about privacy, and the practice was discontinued.

It is worthwhile for companies to address that issue and to explore the potential of empathic-design techniques in the marketspace. Not only is it straightforward and inexpensive to observe customers' behavior in the virtual world, but many companies are already collecting the raw material they need, whether they know it or not, simply by virtue of their ongoing activities in marketspace channels. Every move that consumers make in the virtual world leaves a digital fingerprint; collectively, those prints form a trail that outlines needs and desires, pointing the way toward successful innovation.

Originally Published in November–December 1997
Reprint 97606

Putting Your Company's Whole Brain to Work

DOROTHY LEONARD AND

SUSAAN STRAUS

Executive Summary

INNOVATE OR FALL BEHIND: the competitive imperative for virtually all businesses today is that simple.
Responding to that command is difficult, however,
because innovation takes place when different ideas,
perceptions, and ways of processing and judging information collide. And it often requires collaboration
among players who see the world differently. As a
result, the conflict that should take place constructively
among ideas all too often ends up taking place unproductively among people. Disputes become personal,
and the creative process breaks down.

The manager successful at fostering innovation figures out how to get different approaches to grate
against one another in a productive process the authors
call *creative abrasion*. The authors have worked with a
number of organizations over the years and have

observed many managers who know how to make creative abrasion work for them. Those managers understand that different people have different thinking styles: analytical or intuitive, conceptual or experiential, social or independent, logical or values driven. They deliberately design a full spectrum of approaches and perspectives into their organizations and understand that cognitively diverse people must respect other thinking styles. They set ground rules for working together to discipline the creative process. Above all, managers who want to encourage innovation need to examine what *they* do to promote or inhibit creative abrasion.

INNOVATE OR FALL BEHIND: the competitive imperative for virtually all businesses today is that simple. Achieving it is hard, however, because innovation takes place when different ideas, perceptions, and ways of processing and judging information collide. That, in turn, often requires collaboration among various players who see the world in inherently different ways. As a result, the conflict that should take place constructively among ideas all too often ends up taking place unproductively among people who do not innately understand one another. Disputes become personal, and the creative process breaks down.

Generally, managers have two responses to this phenomenon. On the one hand, managers who dislike conflict—or value only their own approach—actively avoid the clash of ideas. They hire and reward people of a particular stripe, usually people like themselves. Their organizations fall victim to what we call the *comfortable clone syndrome*: coworkers share similar interests and training; everyone thinks alike. Because all ideas pass through similar cognitive screens, only familiar ones survive. For example, a new-business development group formed entirely of employees with the same disciplinary background and set of experiences will assess every idea with an unvarying set of assumptions and analytical tools. Such a group will struggle to innovate, often in vain.

On the other hand, managers who value employees with a variety of thinking styles frequently don't understand how to manage them. They act as if locking a group of diverse individuals in the same room will necessarily result in a creative solution to a problem. They overlook the fact that people with different styles often don't understand or respect one another, and that such differences can fuel personal disagreements. The "detail guy" dismisses the "vision thing"; the "concept man" deplores endless analysis; and the individualist considers the demands of a team an utter waste of time. They simply can't work together without help.

The manager successful at fostering innovation figures out how to get different approaches to grate against one another in a productive process we call *creative abrasion*. Such a manager understands that different people have different thinking styles: analytical or intuitive, conceptual or experiential, social or independent, logical or values driven. She deliberately designs a full spectrum of approaches and perspectives into her organization—whether that organization is a team, a work group, or an entire company—and she understands that cognitively diverse people must respect the thinking styles of others. She sets ground rules for working together to discipline the creative process. Above all, the manager who wants to encourage innovation in her organization needs to examine what she does to promote or inhibit creative abrasion.

We have worked with a number of organizations over the years and have observed many managers who know how to make creative abrasion work for them. In order to create new ideas and products, such managers actively manage the process of bringing together a variety of people who think and act in potentially conflicting ways.

How We Think

What we call *cognitive differences* are varying approaches to perceiving and assimilating data, making decisions, solving problems, and relating to other people. These approaches are *preferences* (not to be confused with skills or abilities). For instance, you may prefer to approach problems intuitively but in fact may be better trained to approach them analytically. Preferences are not rigid: most people can draw on a mixture of approaches and do not live their lives within narrow cognitive boundaries. We often stretch outside the borders of our preferred operating modes if the conditions are right and the stakes are high enough. That said, we all tend to have one or two preferred habits of thought that influence our decision-making styles and our interactions with others—for good or for ill.

We all have preferred habits of thought that influence how we make decisions and interact with others.

The most widely recognized cognitive distinction is between left-brained and right-brained ways of thinking.

This categorization is more powerful metaphorically than it is accurate physiologically; not all the functions commonly associated with the left brain are located on the left side of the cortex and not all so-called right-brained functions are located on the right. Still, the simple description does usefully capture radically different ways of thinking. An analytical, logical, and sequential approach to problem framing and solving (left-brained thinking) clearly differs from an intuitive, values-based, and nonlinear one (right-brained thinking).

Cognitive preferences also reveal themselves in work styles and decision-making activities. Take collaboration as opposed to independence. Some people prefer to work together on solving problems, whereas others prefer to gather, absorb, and process information by themselves. Each type does its best work under different conditions. Or consider thinking as opposed to feeling. Some people evaluate evidence and make decisions through a structured, logical process, whereas others rely on their values and emotions to guide them to the appropriate action.

The list goes on. Abstract thinkers, for instance, assimilate information from a variety of sources, such as books, reports, videos, and conversations. They prefer learning *about* something rather than experiencing it directly. Experiential people, in contrast, get information from interacting directly with people and things. Some people demand quick decisions no matter the issue, whereas others prefer to generate a lot of options no matter the urgency. One type focuses on details, whereas the other looks for the big picture: the relationships and patterns that the data form.

Not surprisingly, people tend to choose professions that reward their own combination of preferences. Their work experience, in turn, reinforces the original preferences and deepens the associated skills. Therefore, one sees very different problem-solving approaches among accountants, entrepreneurs, social workers, and artists. Proof to an engineer, for example, resides in the numbers. But show a page of numerical data to a playwright, and, more persuaded by his intuition, he may well toss it aside. Of course, assessing people's likely approaches to problem solving only by their discipline can be as misleading as using gender or ethnicity as a guide. Within any profession, there are always people whose thinking styles are at odds with the dominant approach.

The best way for managers to assess the thinking styles of the people they are responsible for is to use an established diagnostic instrument as an assessment tool. A well-tested tool is both more objective and more thorough than the impressions of even the most sensitive and observant of managers. Dozens of diagnostic tools and descriptive analyses of human personality have been developed to identify categories of cognitive approaches to problem solving and communication. All the instruments agree on the following basic points:

- Preferences are neither inherently good nor inherently bad. They are assets or liabilities depending on the situation. For example, politicians or CEOs who prefer to think out loud in public create expectations that they sometimes cannot meet; but the person who requires quiet reflection before acting can be a liability in a crisis.

- Distinguishing preferences emerge early in our lives, and strongly held ones tend to remain relatively stable through the years. Thus, for example, those of us who crave certainty are unlikely ever to have an equal love of ambiguity and paradox.

- We can learn to expand our repertoire of behaviors, to act outside our preferred styles. But that is difficult—like writing with the opposite hand.

- Understanding others' preferences helps people communicate and collaborate.

Managers who use instruments with the credibility of the Myers-Briggs Type Indicator (MBTI®) or the Herrmann Brain Dominance Instrument (HBDI) find that their employees accept the outcomes of the tests and use them to improve their processes and behaviors. (See "Identifying How We Think: The Myers-Briggs Type Indicator® and the Herrmann Brain Dominance Instrument" at the end of this article.)

How We Act

All the assessment in the world means nothing unless new understanding brings different actions. Instruments such as the MBTI® and the HBDI will help you understand yourself and will help others understand themselves. The managerial challenge is to use the insights that these instruments offer to create new processes and encourage new behaviors that will help innovation efforts succeed.

Understand yourself. Start with yourself. When you identify your own style, you gain insight into the ways your preferences unconsciously shape your style of leadership and patterns of communication. You may be surprised to discover that your style can stifle the very creativity you seek from your employees. Consider the experiences of two managers of highly creative organizations. Each was at odds with his direct reports—but for very different reasons.

Jim Shaw, executive vice president of MTV Networks, is a left-brained guy in a right-brained organization. Said Shaw:

I have always characterized the creative, right-brained, visionary-type people here as dreamers. What I've realized is that when a dreamer expressed a vision, my gut reaction was to say, 'Well, if you want to do that, what you've got to do is A, then B, then you have to work out C, and because you've got no people and you've got no satellite up-link, you'll have to do D and E.' I've learned that saying that to a creative type is like throwing up on the dream. When I say that stuff too soon, the dreamer personalizes it as an attack. I've learned not *to put all of the things that need to be done on the table initially. I can't just blurt it all out—it makes me look like a naysayer. What I've learned to do is to leak the information gradually, then the dreamer knows that I am meeting him halfway.*

Jerry Hirshberg, president of Nissan Design International, ran into precisely the opposite problem. Hirshberg discovered that some of his employees craved the very kind of structure that he personally abhorred. Before this epiphany, he inundated them with information and expected creativity in return. In short, he tried to manage his employees the way *he* would have wanted to be managed. Hirshberg found, however, that a few individuals reacted to every suggestion with a "yes, but . . ." Initially, he interpreted such hesitancy as an anti-innovation bias. But he eventually realized that some of his employees preferred to have more time both to digest problems and to construct logical approaches to his intuitively derived ideas. Given a bit of extra time, they would return to the project with solid, helpful, and insightful plans for implementation. Ironically, it was their commitment to the success of the initiative that caused the employees to hesitate: they wanted the best possible result. Hirshberg recognized that their contributions were as critical as his own or those of any of the other "right-brainers" in the company.

Both Shaw and Hirshberg came to realize that their own cognitive preferences unconsciously shaped their leadership styles and communication patterns. In fact, their automatic reactions initially stifled the very creativity they sought from their employees. And note that it was just as important for the predominantly right-brained manager to recognize the contributions of the logicians as it was for the left-brained manager to acknowledge the organic approach of the visionaries. Except in theoretical models, creativity is not the exclusive province of one side or the other.

To innovate successfully, you must hire, work with, and promote people who are unlike you.

If you want an innovative organization, you need to hire, work with, and promote people who make you uncomfortable. You need to understand your own preferences so that you can complement your weaknesses and exploit your strengths. The biggest barrier to recognizing the contributions of people who are unlike you is your own ego. Suppose you are stalled on a difficult problem. To whom do you go for help? Usually to someone who is on the same wavelength or to someone whose opinion you respect. These people may give you soothing strokes, but they are unlikely to help spark a new idea. Suppose you were to take the problem instead to someone with whom you often find yourself at odds, someone who rarely validates your ideas or perspectives. It may take courage and tact to get constructive feedback, and the process may not be exactly pleasant. But that feedback will likely improve the quality of your solution. And when your adversary recovers from his amazement at your request, he may even get along with you better because the disagreement was clearly intellectual, not personal.

Forget the golden rule. Don't treat people the way you want to be treated. Tailor communications to the receiver instead of the sender. In a cognitively diverse environment, a message sent is not necessarily a message received. Some people respond well to facts, figures, and statistics. Others prefer anecdotes. Still others digest graphic presentations most easily. Information must be delivered in the preferred "language" of the recipient if it is to be received at all.

For example, say you want to persuade an organization to adopt an open office layout. Arguments appealing to the analytical mind would rely on statistics from well-documented research conducted by objective experts that prove that open architecture enhances the effectiveness of communication. Arguments geared toward the action-oriented type would answer specific questions about implementation: How long will the office conversion take? Exactly what kind of furniture is needed? What are the implications for acoustics? Arguments aimed at people-oriented individuals would focus on such questions as, How does an open office affect relationships? How would this setup affect morale? and Are people happy in this sort of setup?

In a cognitively diverse environment, a message sent is not necessarily a message received.

Arguments crafted for people with a future-oriented perspective would include graphics as well as artists' renderings of the proposed environment. In short, regardless of how you personally would prefer to deliver the message, you will be more persuasive and better understood if you formulate messages to appeal to the particular thinking style of your listener.

Create "whole-brained" teams. Either over time or by initial design, company or group cultures can become dominated by one particular cognitive style. IBM, in the days when it was known as "Big Blue," presented a uniform face to the world; Digital Equipment prided itself on its engineering culture. Such homogeneity makes for efficient functioning—and limited approaches to problems or opportunities. Companies with strong cultures can indeed be very creative, but within predictable boundaries: say, clever marketing or imaginative engineering. When the market demands that such companies innovate in different ways, they have to learn new responses. Doing so requires adopting a variety of approaches to solving a problem—using not just the right brain or the left brain but the *whole* brain.

Consider the all-too-common error made by John, a rising star in a large, diversified instrument company: he forfeited an important career opportunity because he failed to see the need for a whole-brained team. Appointed manager of a new-product development group, John had a charter to bring in radically innovative ideas for products and services for launch in three to six years. "Surprise me," the CEO said.

Given a free hand in hiring, John lured in three of the brightest M.B.A.'s he could find. They immediately went to work conducting industry analyses and sorting through existing product possibilities, applying their recently acquired skills in financial analysis. To complete the team, John turned to the pile of résumés on his desk sent to him by human resources. All the applicants had especially strong quantitative skills, and a couple were engineers. John was pleased. Surely a group of such intelligent, well-trained, rigorous thinkers would be able to come up with some radical innovations for the company. Ignoring advice to hire some right-brained people to stimulate different ideas, he continued to populate his group with left-brained wizards. After 18 months, the team had rejected all the proposed new projects in the pipeline on the basis of well-argued and impressively documented financial and technical risk analysis. But the team's members had not come up with a single new idea. The CEO was neither surprised nor pleased, and the group was disbanded just short of its second anniversary.

In contrast, Bob, a successful entrepreneur embarking on his latest venture, resisted the strong temptation to tolerate only like-minded people. He knew from his prior ventures that his highly analytical style alienated some of his most creative people. Despite his unusual degree of self-awareness, Bob came within a hair's breadth of firing a strong and experienced manager: Wally, his director of human resources. According to Bob, after several months on board, Wally appeared to be "a quart and a half low." Why? Because he was inattentive in budget meetings and focused on what Bob perceived as trivia—day care, flextime, and benefits. Before taking action, however, Bob decided to look at the management team through the lens of thinking styles. He soon realized that Wally was exactly the kind of person he needed to help him grow his small company. Wally contributed a key element that was otherwise missing in the management team: a sensitivity to human needs that helped the company foresee and forestall problems with employees. So Bob learned to meet Wally halfway. Describing his success in learning to work with Wally, he told us, "You would have been proud of me. I started our meetings with five minutes of dogs, kids, and station wagons." Although the concern Wally demonstrated for the workers in the company did not eliminate union issues completely, it did minimize antagonism toward management and made disputes easier to resolve.

The list of whole-brained teams that continue to innovate successfully is long. At Xerox PARC, social scientists work alongside computer scientists. For instance, computer scientist Pavel Curtis, who is creating a virtual world in which people will meet and mingle, is working with an anthropologist who understands how communities form. As a result, Curtis's cyberspace meeting places have more human touches and are more welcoming than they would have been had they been designed only by scientists. Another example is the PARC PAIR (PARC Artist In Residence) program, which links computer scientists with artists so that each may influence the other's perceptions and representations of the world. At Interval Research, a California think tank dedicated to multimedia technologies, Director David Liddle invites leaders from various disciplines to visit for short "sabbaticals." The purpose is to stimulate a cross-fertilization of ideas and approaches to solving problems. The resulting exchanges have helped Interval Research create and spin off several highly innovative start-ups. And Jerry Hirshberg applies the whole-brain principle to hiring practices at Nissan Design by bringing designers into his organization in virtual pairs. That is, when he hires a designer who glories in the freedom of pure color and rhythm, he will next hire a very rational, Bauhaus-trained designer who favors analysis and focuses on function.

Complete homogeneity in an organization's cognitive approach can be very efficient. But as managers at Xerox PARC, Interval Research, and Nissan Design have learned, no matter how brilliant the group of individuals, their contributions to innovative problem solving are enhanced by coming up against totally different perspectives.

Look for the ugly duckling. Suppose you don't have the luxury of hiring new people yet find your organization mired in a swamp of stale thinking patterns. Consider the experience of the CEO of the U.S. subsidiary of a tightly controlled and conservative European chemical company. Even though the company's business strategy had never worked well in the United States, headquarters pushed the CEO to do more of the same. He knew he needed to figure out a fresh approach because the U.S. company was struggling to compete in a rapidly changing marketplace. But his direct reports were as uniformly left-brained as his superiors in Europe and were disinclined to work with him to figure out new solutions.

Rather than give up, the CEO tested thinking preferences further down in the organization. He found the cognitive disparity that he needed in managers one layer below his direct reports—a small but dynamic set of individuals whose countercultural thinking patterns had constrained their advancement. In this company, people with right-brained preferences were seen as helpful but were not considered top management material. They were never promoted above a certain level.

The CEO changed that. He elevated three managers with right-brained proclivities to the roles of senior vice president and division head—lofty positions occupied until then exclusively by left-brained individuals. The new executives were strong supporters of the CEO's intentions to innovate and worked with him to develop new approaches to the business. They understood that their communication strategy with headquarters would be critical to their success. They deliberately packaged their new ideas in a way that appealed to the cognitive framework of their European owner. Instead of lecturing about the need to change and try new ideas as they had in the past, the Americans presented their ideas as ways of solving problems. They supported their positions with well-researched quantitative data and with calculated anticipated cost savings and ROI—and described how similar approaches had succeeded elsewhere. They detailed the specific steps they would follow to succeed. Within two years, the U.S. subsidiary embarked on a major organizational redesign effort that included such radical notions as permitting outside competition for internal services. The quality of internal services soared—as did the number of innovations generated by the company in the United States.

Manage the creative process. Abrasion is not creative unless managers make it so. Members of whole-brained teams don't naturally understand one another, and they can easily come to dislike one another. Successful managers of richly diverse groups spend time from the outset getting members to acknowledge their

differences—often through a joint exploration of the
results of a diagnostic analysis—and devise guidelines
for working together before attempting to act on the
problem at hand. Managers who find it awkward or
difficult to lead their groups in identifying cognitive
styles or in establishing guidelines can usually enlist the
aid of someone who is trained in facilitation.

People often feel a bit foolish creating rules about
how they will work together. Surely, the thinking goes,
we are all adults and have years of experience in deal-
ing with group dynamics.

Successful managers spend time getting members of diverse groups to acknowledge their differences.

That, of course, is the problem. Everyone has practiced
dysfunctional behavior for
years. We learn to value
politeness over truth at our
mothers' knees. (Who hasn't
mastered the art of the white lie by age 16?) We often
discount an argument if it has an element of emotion
or passion. We opt out if we feel ignored—people with
unappreciated thinking styles learn to sit against the
wall during meetings (the organizational back-of-the-
bus). And we usually don't even notice those behaviors
because they are so routine.

But the cost of allowing such behaviors to overtake a
group is too high. Bob Meyers, senior vice president of
interactive media at NBC, uses a sports analogy to make
the point: "On a football team, for example, you have to
use all kinds of people. Like the little, skinny guy who
can only kick the ball. He may not even look as if he
belongs on the team. This guy can't stand up to the
refrigerator types that play in other positions. But as
long as he does his job, he doesn't need to be big. He can

just do what he does best. The catch is that the team needs to recognize what the little skinny guy can do—or they lose the benefit of his talent."

Managing the process of creative abrasion means making sure that everyone is at the front of the bus and talking. Some simple but powerful techniques can be helpful. First, clarify why you are working together by keeping the common goal in front of the group at all times. "If the goal is a real-world one with shared accountability and timetables attached," one manager observed, "then everyone understands the relevance of honoring one another's differences."

Second, make your operating guidelines explicit. Effective guidelines are always simple, clear, and concise. For example, one group set up the following principles about handling disagreements: "Anyone can disagree about anything with anyone, but no one can disagree without stating the reason" and "When someone states an objection, everyone else should listen to it, try to understand it, treat it as legitimate, and counter with their reasons if they don't agree with it." Some principles are as simple as "discuss taboo subjects," "verify assumptions," and "arrive on time with your homework done."

> *Managing the process of creative abrasion means making sure that everyone in the group is talking.*

Third, set up an agenda ahead of time that explicitly provides enough time for both *divergent* discussion to uncover imaginative alternatives and *convergent* discussion to select an option and plan its implementation. Innovation requires both types of discussion,

but people who excel at different types can, as one
manager observed, "drive each other nuts." Another
manager said, "If you ask people comfortable with
ambiguity whether they prefer A or B, they will ask,
'How about C?'" Meanwhile, the people who crave closure will be squirming in their seats at the seemingly
pointless discussion. Moreover, if one approach domi-
nates, the unbalanced group process can risk
producing an unacceptable or unfeasible new product,
service, or change. Clearly allocating time to the two
different types of discussion will contain the frustra-
tions of both the decisive types, who are constantly
looking at their watches wanting the decision to be
made now, and the ambiguous types, who want to be
sure that all possible avenues for creativity have been
explored. Otherwise, the decisive members generally
will pound the others into silence by invoking time
pressures and scheduling. They will grab the first
viable option rather than the best one. Or if the less
decisive dominate, the group may never reach a conclusion. Innovation requires both divergent and convergent thinking, both brainstorming and action plans.

Depersonalize conflict. Diverse cognitive preferences
can cause tremendous tensions in any group, yet innovation requires the cross-fertilization of ideas. And
because many new products are systems rather than
stand-alone pieces, many business projects cannot pro-
ceed without the cooperation of people who receive different messages from the same words and make different observations about the same incidents. The single
most valuable contribution that understanding different
thinking and communication styles brings to the pro-

cess of innovation is taking the sting out of intellectual disagreements that turn personal.

Consider the experience of the product manager of a radically new product for a medical supplies company. Facing a strict deadline of just 14 months to design and deliver a new surgical instrument, the manager's team needed to pull together fast. Design felt misled by marketing, however, and manufacturing couldn't understand design's delay in choosing between two mechanical hinges. The disagreements turned personal, starting with "you always . . ." and ending with "irresponsible ignorance." Two months into the project, the manager began to wonder whether he should disband the team and start over again. But he knew that his boss, the vice president of marketing, would not agree to extend the deadline. "I was desperate," he recalled. "I decided to make one last attempt at getting them to work together."

The manager decided to experiment with an off-site gathering of his staff, including sessions diagnosing cognitive preferences. When they returned to work, the team members used the new language they had learned to label their differences in opinion and style. "At first, using the terms was kind of a joke," the manager recalled. "They'd say things like, 'Well, of course I want the schedule right now. I'm a J!' Yet you could tell that people were really seeing one another in a different light, and they weren't getting angry." The team made its deadline; perhaps even more important, several members voluntarily joined forces to work on the next iteration of the product. This willingness to work together generated more value for the company than just "warm fuzzies." Critical technical knowledge was preserved in one small, colocated group—knowledge that would have

been scattered had project members dispersed to different product lines. Moreover, keeping part of the team
together resulted in a rapid development time for the
derivative product.

People who do not understand cognitive preferences
tend to personalize conflict or avoid it—or both. The
realization that another person's approach is not wrong-
headed and stubborn, but merely predictably different,
diffuses anger. For example, at Viacom, a planning session involving two managers had ground to a halt. One
manager simply wouldn't buy into the idea that the other
was presenting. Suddenly, the presenter slapped his head
and said, "Oooohhh! I get it! You're left-brained! Give me
half an hour to switch gears, and I'll be right back. Let me
try this one more time." The left-brained manager laugh-
ingly agreed—he understood the paradigm—and the
meeting resumed with the presenter armed with quantitative data and a much more cohesive and logical presen-
tation. Establishing that kind of effective two-way
communication led to a common understanding of the
issues at hand and, ultimately, a solution.

Understanding that someone views a problem differently does not mean you will agree. But an important
element in understanding thinking styles is recognizing
that no one style is inherently better than another. Each
style brings a uniquely valuable perspective to the process of innovation, just as each style has some negatives
associated with it. Stereotypes of the cold-hearted logi-
cian, the absent-minded, creative scientist, and the
bleeding-heart liberal have some basis in reality. If
people even partially internalize the inherent value of
different perspectives, they will take disagreements less
personally and will be better able to argue and reach a
compromise or a consensus with less animosity. They

will be open to the possibility that an alien view of the world might actually enhance their own. They will be better equipped to listen for the "a-ha" that occurs at the intersection of different planes of thought.

Caveat Emptor

Personality analysis of the type we describe is no more than a helpful tool, and it has many limitations. The diagnostic instruments measure only one aspect of personality: preferences in thinking styles and communication. They do not measure ability or intelligence, and they do not predict performance. Neither the MBTI® nor the HBDI measure other qualities that are critical to successful innovation such as courage, curiosity, integrity, empathy, or drive.

Preferences tend to be relatively stable, but life experiences can affect them. For example, repeated application of the MBTI® over a period of years has revealed a tendency for people to drift from a thinking style toward a feeling style when they have children. For the most part, however, studies done with both the MBTI® and the HBDI suggest that people retain their dominant preferences throughout a variety of work and social circumstances.

One critical warning label should be attached to any of these diagnostic instruments: only trained individuals should administer them. Not only can results be incorrectly interpreted (for instance, what are intended to be neutral descriptions of preferences might be labeled "right" or "wrong" behavior), but they can also be misused to invade people's privacy or to stereotype them. Of course, it is a human tendency to simplify in order to comprehend complexities; we stereotype people all the time on the basis of their language, dress, and behavior. Because these diagnostics have the weight of considerable psychological research behind them, however, they can be dangerous when misused. Without structured, reliable diagnoses, judgments are likely to be superficial and flawed. And without a substantial investment of time and resources, managers can't expect abrasion to be creative.

ONE OF THE PARADOXES of modern management is that, in the midst of technical and social change so pervasive and rapid that it seems out of pace with the rhythms of nature, human personality has not altered throughout recorded history. People have always had distinct preferences in their approaches to problem solving. Why then is it only now becoming so necessary for managers to understand those differences? Because today's complex products demand integrating the expertise of individuals who do not innately understand one another. Today's pace of change demands that these individuals quickly develop the ability to work together. If abrasion is not managed into creativity, it will constrict the constructive impulses of individuals and organizations alike. Rightly harnessed, the energy released by the intersection of different thought processes will propel innovation.

Identifying How We Think: The Myers-Briggs Type Indicator

THE MYERS-BRIGGS TYPE INDICATOR (MBTI®) is the most widely used personality-assessment instrument in the world. Designed by a mother-and-daughter team, Isabel Myers and her mother Katherine Cook Briggs, the MBTI® is based on the work of Carl Jung. Myers and Briggs developed the instrument during World War II on the hypothesis that an understanding of personality preferences might aid those civilians who were entering the workforce for the first time to find the right job for the war effort. The instrument conforms to standard testing conventions and, at last count in 1994, had been taken by more than two and a half million people around the world. The MBTI® is widely used in business, psychology, and education, as well as in career counseling.

The MBTI® uses four different pairs of attributes to create a matrix of 16 personality types:

- Extraversion versus Introversion.[1] The first pair looks at where people prefer to focus their attention. These E/I descriptors focus on the source of someone's mental energy: extraverts draw energy from other people; introverts draw energy from themselves. Each finds the other's preferred operating conditions enervating.

- Sensing versus "Intuition." The second pair identifies how one absorbs information. "Sensors" (S) gather data through their five senses, whereas "Intuitives" (N) rely on less direct perceptions, such as patterns, relationships, and hunches. For example, when asked to describe the same painting, a group of S's might comment on the brush strokes or the scar on the subject's left cheek, whereas a group of N's might imagine from the troubled look in the subject's eyes that he lived in difficult times or suffered from depression.

- Thinking versus Feeling. The third pair measures how one makes decisions once information is gathered. Feeling types (F) use their emotional intelligence to make decisions based on values—their internal sense of right and

The MBTI®

		Sensing Types (S)	
		Thinking (T)	**Feeling (F)**
Introverts (I)	**Judging (J)**	**ISTJ** Serious, quiet, earn success by concentration and thorough- ness. Practical, orderly, matter- of-fact, logical, realistic, and dependable. Take responsibility.	**ISFJ** Quiet, friendly, responsible, and conscientious. Work devotedly to meet their obligations. Thor- ough, painstaking, accurate. Loyal, considerate.
	Perceiving (P)	**ISTP** Cool onlookers—quiet, reserved, and analytical. Usually inter- ested in impersonal principles, how and why mechanical things work. Flashes of original humor.	**ISFP** Retiring, quietly friendly, sensitive, kind, modest about their abilities. Shun disagreements. Loyal fol- lowers. Often relaxed about get- ting things done.
Extraverts (E)	**Perceiving (P)**	**ESTP** Matter-of-fact, do not worry or hurry, enjoy whatever comes along. May be a bit blunt or insensitive. Best with real things that can be taken apart or put together.	**ESFP** Outgoing, easygoing, accepting, friendly, make things fun for others by their enjoy- ment. Like sports and making things. Find remembering facts easier than mastering theories.
	Judging (J)	**ESTJ** Practical, realistic, matter-of-fact, with a natural head for business or mechanics. Not interested in subjects they see no use for. Like to organize and run activities.	**ESFJ** Warm-hearted, talkative, popu- lar, conscientious, born cooper- ators. Need harmony. Work best with encouragement. Little interest in abstract thinking or technical subjects.

Intuitive Types (N)			
Feeling (F)	**Thinking (T)**		
INFJ Succeed by perseverance, originality, and desire to do whatever is needed or wanted. Quietly forceful, conscientious, concerned for others. Respected for their firm principles.	**INTJ** Usually have original minds and great drive for their own ideas and purposes. Skeptical, critical, independent, determined, often stubborn.	Judging (J)	Introverts (I)
INFP Care about learning, ideas, language, and independent projects of their own. Tend to undertake too much, then somehow get it done. Friendly, but often too absorbed.	**INTP** Quiet, reserved, impersonal. Enjoy theoretical or scientific subjects. Usually interested mainly in ideas, little liking for parties or small talk. Sharply defined interests.	Perceiving (P)	
ENFP Warmly enthusiastic, high-spirited, ingenious, imaginative. Able to do almost anything that interests them. Quick with a solution and to help with a problem.	**ENTP** Quick, ingenious, good at many things. May argue either side of a question for fun. Resourceful in solving challenging problems, but may neglect routine assignments.	Perceiving (P)	Extraverts (E)
ENFJ Responsive and responsible. Generally feel real concern for what others think or want. Sociable, popular. Sensitive to praise and criticism.	**ENTJ** Hearty, frank, decisive, leaders. Usually good at anything that requires reasoning and intelligent talk. May sometimes be more positive than their experience in an area warrants.	Judging (J)	

wrong. Thinking types (T) tend to make decisions based on logic and "objective" criteria—their assessment of truth and falsehood.

- Judging versus Perceiving. The fourth pair describes how a person is oriented toward the outer world. Judging types (J) have a high need for closure. They reach conclusions quickly based on available data and move on. Perceiving types (P) prefer to keep their options open. They wait until they have gathered what they consider to be enough information to decide. J's crave certainty, and P's love ambiguity.

To read descriptions of the personality types identified in the MBTI®, see the matrix on the lower right.

The Herrmann Brain Dominance Instrument

NED HERRMANN CREATED and developed the Herrmann Brain Dominance Instrument (HBDI)[2] while he was a manager at General Electric. Starting his research with large groups within GE, he expanded it over 20 years through tens of thousands of surveys and has validated the data with prominent psychometric research institutions, including the Educational Testing Service.

The HBDI measures a person's preference both for right-brained or left-brained thinking and for conceptual or experiential thinking. These preferences often correspond to specific professions. Engineers, for example, consistently describe themselves as analytical, mathematical, and logical, placing them on the left end of the continuum. Artists, in contrast, describe themselves as emotional, spatial, and aesthetic, placing them on the right end of the continuum.

The charts below show how the different preferences combine into four distinct quadrants and how one can use the chart to analyze teams with different cognitive preferences:

Composite One: The Homogeneous Team

The chart below shows that everyone in the group approaches problems and challenges with the same emphasis on correctness. As engineers, the members of the team know how to do things correctly. Although the quality of their work is excellent, the members are difficult to work with. They have their own ways of doing things, and they reject variations from set standards. As a corporate function, the team has long enjoyed a captive audience in the company. Recently, members found themselves in trouble when the company restructured and other functions in the organization were allowed to outsource engineering.

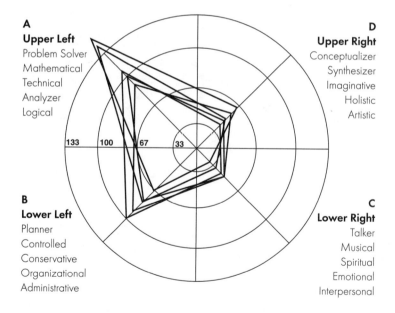

A
Upper Left
Problem Solver
Mathematical
Technical
Analyzer
Logical

133 100 67 33

B
Lower Left
Planner
Controlled
Conservative
Organizational
Administrative

D
Upper Right
Conceptualizer
Synthesizer
Imaginative
Holistic
Artistic

C
Lower Right
Talker
Musical
Spiritual
Emotional
Interpersonal

Composite Two: *The Heterogeneous Team*

The Management Services Group includes managers from information technology, the mail room, and the cafeteria. Although members share such goals as an orientation toward quality, they encounter a wide range of business problems. The manager's dominant thinking style is in the lower right quadrant: a natural facilitator, she develops people, listens empathetically, and fosters a spirit of respect among her reports. Her leadership unified what had been a fragmented, inefficient collection of functions. Members regard one another as resources, enjoy the group's diversity, and take pride in their work.

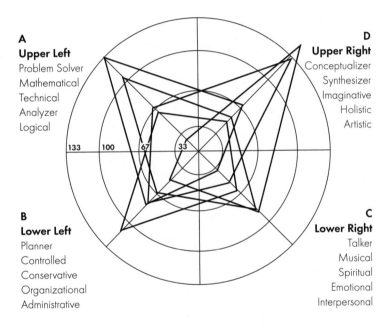

A
Upper Left
Problem Solver
Mathematical
Technical
Analyzer
Logical

133 100 67 33

D
Upper Right
Conceptualizer
Synthesizer
Imaginative
Holistic
Artistic

B
Lower Left
Planner
Controlled
Conservative
Organizational
Administrative

C
Lower Right
Talker
Musical
Spiritual
Emotional
Interpersonal

Notes

1. MBTI® preferred spelling.

2. For more information, please contact Herrmann International, 794 Buffalo Creek Road, Lake Lure, NC 28746 (http://www.hbdi.com).

Originally published in July–August 1997
Reprint 97407

A Film Director's Approach to Managing Creativity

EILEEN MORLEY AND ANDREW SILVER

Executive Summary

WHEN A FILM DIRECTOR SAYS "action" and the actors and technicians begin a take, what is happening? To most of us, "action" simply means Hollywood. But to the actors and technicians, "action" means "get to work." Despite their glamour, film units are work systems. Their purpose is the production of a film—a task that relies on talented people banding together for a short time. In many ways, film units are similar to scientific and consulting projects; their success depends on getting the right personnel, enabling them to begin working together well and quickly, motivating them, leading them to create on schedule, and handling the stresses that working in isolation can create. The authors studied a film being made and how the director created his product and handled these problems. The film they studied was *Night Moves* (1975). The director was Arthur Penn, who is probably

best known for his films *Bonnie and Clyde* (1967), *Little
Big Man* (1970), and *Missouri Breaks* (1976). Gene
Hackman, who won an Academy Award for *The French
Connection*, starred in the film.

WHEN SOMEONE MENTIONS a film unit, most
people think of location shooting—depending on their
generation it's either Robert Shaw duelling the shark
off Martha's Vineyard or John Wayne and the U.S. cav-
alry charging through Death Valley! But, in fact, most
major films are made in a series of predictable phases,
of which shooting is only one.

In each phase of a film's production a group of people
collaborate to form a miniature work organization
which has characteristic problems of motivation, leadership, and structure. Each phase is a temporary system,
limited in duration and membership, in which people
come together, interact, create something, and then disband. And in each phase, the director has to stimulate
and manage different kinds of creative work under
intense budget and time pressures. The director's princi-
pal job is managing the creative process.

In this article we use the word "creativity" to mean
technical as well as artistic creativity, realizing that this
will overlap what others define as innovation. The
notion of creativity is important because there is a high
correlation between temporariness and creativity; and
between permanence and routine. Most temporary organizations, such as film units or project teams, exist to
develop an idea, a plan, a product, or a service, or to
make something happen such as a trip to the moon or a
bicentennial celebration. When groups or teams have

completed their task, they dissolve. In contrast, permanent organizations exist to carry out a relatively repetitive manufacturing or service task for which there is a continuing need.

Because film units are temporary creative systems, they have much in common with technical or scientific projects, consulting teams, task forces, and other short-term task groups. For this reason observations about the film unit we studied should be relevant to managers of such groups.

Film units go through three main phases. Each involves different people, tasks, and locations. Only the director, producer, and script writer stay with the process from start to finish. But before anything can begin, a deal has to be made—a package of writer (and script), a director, and "bankable" star, all of whom are committed, and whose commitment forms the basis of the deal. Putting the package together is like developing a proposal; getting the package financed is akin to getting the contract. Once this has happened, the film unit comes into existence.

The first phase (preproduction) consists of script development, production planning, casting, and hiring. The preproduction team is usually small, consisting mainly of people who are close to and trusted by the director.

The production phase involves the actual shooting of the film. This phase usually has a visible social structure and culture of its own. People are separated into occupational groups or subsystems: actors, camera crew, lighting crew, sound crew, and so on. They are also divided into two levels: "above-the-line" and "below-the-line." The line is literally a line on a budget sheet. The main philosophic difference between the groups is in their sense of responsibility. Above-the-line people tend to be committed to the film as a whole. They include the "management group" (producer, director, and script writer), and the key actors. Below-the-line people, such as members of the technical crews, carpenters, drivers, and so on, tend to be committed only to a particular aspect of the film.

The postproduction phase begins when the production group has disbanded. It includes picture and sound editing and recording and synchronizing of music and other sound effects. Usually the postproduction phase resembles the preproduction one in that during each a small group of people work in close contact with one another and the director. There is usually also a subsequent marketing phase, but since the parent studio organization carries this out after completion of the film and the film unit itself is not involved, we did not include it in our study.

Most temporary projects go through an analogous series of phases. The people who plan and recruit an operation are not necessarily the ones who implement or lead it; nor again are the ones who implement it the ones who follow up, or even clean up. The most useful way to analyze the phases is by examining membership. Who belongs? At what time and for what purpose does each person belong? For how long? Which sets of people have to work well together? How will people be grouped and how will they group themselves? How will the groupings change as the project moves from phase to phase?

Few managers think about the systems they lead as social organizations of this kind, or about the key roles and interfaces between individuals, groups, and levels. However, the structural characteristics of a work system have a great influence on communication and collaboration. People who work together or see each other informally tend to exchange information and form relationships—people who come on line before or after each other, or who work in separate buildings, do not.

In this article we describe the life cycle of the film unit, and consider in more detail some of the processes and problems that are common to the management of any temporary system.

Planning the Film

The film we studied was *Night Moves*, directed by Arthur Penn and starring Gene Hackman and Susan Clark. The preproduction of *Night Moves* took place in Los Angeles, where a small "family" group worked in contiguous offices with much face-to-face contact and informal consultation. Hours were long and the atmosphere was very personal, much like the atmosphere of any small group getting together to start up a new project.

One of the main tasks of the preproduction group was to recruit people for the crucial production phase to follow. Recruiting of actors was more than unusually important because Arthur Penn's concept of film making centers on creating and filming an authentic spontaneous happening in the acting process; not on capturing the repetition of some previously rehearsed behavior. Because it was critical to find actors who could really give Penn what he wanted, Gene Lasko, the associate producer, did the casting, instead of leaving it up to a casting agency or the casting department of the parent company, as usually happens.

Four main actors were chosen to go through screen tests, which Penn used to generate photographic data

that he could examine at leisure in making casting decisions. Penn was interested in the actors' professional
competence and style; their stamina, patience, and willingness to follow instructions; their ability to remain
spontaneous after ten takes of the same few lines of dialogue; their response to stress and fatigue; and their
reactions to his way of working, which differs from that
of many directors. The screen tests enabled him to make
an in-depth assessment of the actors before committing
himself.

Robert Sherman, the producer, and Tom Schmidt, the
production manager, recruited the technical personnel,
also with great care. They hired some of the technical
personnel in groups. For instance, the directors of photography, lighting, and sound brought their own crews
with them. Sherman and Schmidt were not only seeking
people with professional competence, but also people
with the ability to commit themselves quickly to a short
project, and to tolerate stress ("Don't take him; he gets
upset and lays it on everyone else").

They looked for people known to have a helpful,
responsible attitude ("If I help him, they'll bend over
even more to help me"). Most of all they wanted people
who would not get "uptight." All these qualities were
explored through firsthand knowledge, word-of-mouth
reputation, and conversations with other people in the
business. Sherman and Schmidt's search for people with
the correct qualities was more persistent than is customary in business or recruiting.

Because the film industry is based almost completely
on temporary systems, and because the success of any
film depends at least as much on compatibility and
interpersonal skills as on technical performance, the
emphasis on interpersonal compatibility was taken for

granted by everyone. This emphasis is not likely to be so evident in a business or industrial situation where the norms and cultural expectations have been drawn from traditional permanent organizations which value technical above interpersonal competence.

The project manager who sensibly tries to assess the people he is recruiting in terms of their compatibility and tolerance for stress may have to develop a language in which to communicate his inquiries. "Does so-and-so ever lose his temper? How does he behave then?" "Is she sensitive and responsive to other people's feelings?" "How does he react when he's given an impossible workload or conflicting instructions?" "Does she have a sense of humor?" "Does the quality of his work deteriorate badly under pressure?" "Can she see someone else's point of view?

Managers who attempt to broaden their recruiting procedures in this way encounter occasional criticism of their "hairsplitting" or "inappropriately personal" questions. Inquiries of this kind can usually only be made in a phone call or face-to-face conversation with a previous supervisor, who in turn may have difficulty in formulating a reply, even if he or she is trying to do so. Exploring how people stack up on these counts is extremely time-consuming, but it is as essential to high-pressure technical projects as it is to a film unit if the project is to have the best chance of success.

In the business world there is no equivalent of the screen tests, which Penn used to evaluate the people he was proposing to hire. Permanent organizations do employ people "on probation," but in temporary systems there is rarely time for this. Nonetheless, it is possible for a manager or section leader to keep a close eye on the more critical members of the team during the project's early days; to set particular technical or interpersonal tasks for them; to see how they respond; and to make an early decision to terminate those who do not measure up. Selection and early testing are even more important, simply because there will not be time to find and train a substitute later on.

Unfortunately, business people are more ready to accept lack of technical ability than lack of interpersonal skill as a reason for replacing someone. Business people tend to cling to the notion that somehow a good manager should be able to turn a difficult industrial or unsatisfactory subordinate around. But on short-term projects managers usually do not have the time to help people go through a process of change. At the same time, however, it is important that they find the time to acknowledge the skills and contributions of the more effective people early, so that these people quickly feel valued and committed to the task.

The Shooting

Night Moves' production phase, in which about 70 people were involved, took place in studios in Los Angeles and on location in Florida. The shift from preproduction to production was a substantial one. From being a small group with informal close relationships, the unit metamorphosed into a much larger organization with a more complex structure. Different subgroups had to be brought into working relationships. Different levels of understanding about what the director wanted had to be brought into equilibrium. Strangers had to become colleagues and perhaps friends.

During the production phase of a film unit there are five main areas of concern that are common to all creative temporary systems. These include the need for people to get into a relationship quickly with the task and with each other; the cultivation of enthusiasm and commitment; the encouragement of creativity; the question of an effective leadership style on the part of the group's head; and the effective management of stress and conflict.

WORKING RELATIONSHIPS

Everyone in the film industry is used to moving into a new production, and takes it for granted that he or she must cultivate working relationships fast. Because they had done it often before, most people in the unit we studied were very skillful at this. In addition, Penn's preference for preproduction rehearsal, as well as certain other structural aspects of the work, helped people get to know each other quickly.

Penn had scheduled a week of rehearsal time at the end of the preproduction phase, which was an unusual thing to do. During production, actors would not all work together at the same time. The rehearsal week had enabled Penn and the cast to experience themselves as a team. It gave actors the chance to learn and develop confidence in Penn's way of working without being under the pressure of the shooting schedule. Actors thought this rehearsal was so important that they agreed to work the rehearsal week at the union scale of pay, which was far below the salary rate for which they had contracted to do the rest of the film.

Another characteristic that accelerates the team process is the isolation that is typical of the studio production process, and which Penn particularly insisted on during rehearsal week. People worked intensively together without any interruptions for hours at a time. The isolation increased concentration on the task and the intensity of personal interaction. It enabled a great deal of work to be done in a relatively short time. This way of working is very stimulating to participants, but it is also extremely tiring. Such intensity can usually be maintained only for short periods and is, therefore, best scheduled immediately before the main task is to begin.

On any project, the development of task familiarity and good working relationships takes a formal commitment of time and money. Usually this process calls for the manager's active participation, not only because of his or her central involvement in the project, but also because, as a signal from management, this will show that the process itself is to be taken seriously. For instance, no ringing phone ever broke people's concentration during rehearsal week. Penn had forbidden all telephone calls during working hours, including his own.

In the business and industrial world, initial socialization of this kind is often skimped or neglected. The process can be formal or informal and can center on task and on personal working relationships or both. Formal task-centered sessions such as orientations, briefings, planning meetings, and so on, give people a chance to develop a sense of their manager as a person, of his or her expectations and concepts of the project, of his or her ways of working. Unless they have had a chance to discuss the task with each person, managers cannot assume that people know what is expected of them.

It is harder to specify what the informal opportunities are for socialization in any particular group. "Shooting the breeze" in the early days of a project is often a valuable way of developing relationships, and is not simply time-wasting, even though it may look like it. All

temporary systems tend to build up their own minicul-
ture of jokes, language, and shared experiences which
can only happen as people interact. In the film unit production phase, the minicultures developed automatically
during the two meals a day that people ate together, and
in the waiting periods between setups. Other temporary
systems don't have such useful interstices of time built
into their structure. Socializing has to occur in other
ways, such as at lunch, in carpools, in conversations in
the washroom, or around the water cooler.

Sometimes wives and husbands also need to be
involved in temporary projects, particularly if later periods of stress are predictable. At these times workers will
need support and understanding from spouses of whom
they've seen too little. Because it is relatively easy for the
husband or wife of an actor or cameraman to understand the product, film units have a distinct advantage
over technical projects in this respect. On projects where
the work is either classified or incomprehensible to the
layperson, managers may need to make special efforts to
involve spouses.

Last, but certainly not least, is the matter of the local
organizational climate. Management does not always
accept the fact that time for people to develop good relationships is an appropriate use of resources. Even where
it is accepted, some methods will be more acceptable
and seem more natural than others, both in the organization at large and among the people who are being
recruited to the temporary project. If the idea of such
preparation is completely unusual, the group may have
to adopt a low profile to prevent its appearing either to
be an elite or in need of special nursing.

Once a manager has developed a sense of the likely
structure of his temporary system, he or she can plan

much of this socialization process in the abstract. When the group convenes, he or she can make readjustments according to the specific characteristics of the people who have been recruited or assigned to the project.

SOURCES OF MOTIVATION

The film director has none of the rewards and penalties traditionally available to the manager of a permanent system. Because so many above-the-line people are indispensable to completion of the film, the director cannot usually transfer or terminate them, and because the roles and responsibilities have been contracted in advance, he or she cannot promote or give raises or improve fringe benefits.

For *Night Moves,* indispensability was highest and most obvious in the case of Gene Hackman, the star, whose life throughout production was insured for the cost of the film to date. But indispensability was not limited to actors. In the technical area, even the footage shot by the regular director of photography had a different look from footage shot by a subordinate while the director was sick.

Managers of all temporary systems share many of these constraints. Many project managers do influence the later careers of staff who continue to work in the same organization in their periodic performance evaluations. But managers do not usually have full administrative authority for raises or terminations. On complex technical tasks, a good many people may be indispensable, either because their expertise is irreplaceable or because tight schedules and deadlines mean there is no time to replace them. In these circumstances, the project manager, like the film director, must depend on four sources of motivation:

1. *A sense of professionalism*—By this we mean commitment to the standards for task and personal behavior set by professional peers inside and outside the system. Where the manager shares the same standards or those of a closely related discipline, he or she can often act as a natural pace-setter.

2. *The basic need to exercise competence*—The opportunity to use existing knowledge, to develop ideas, and to learn something new, gives most people a sense of competence and satisfaction, which in turn strengthens their motivation. However, the opportunity to exercise competence requires a fairly precise definition of the job, a good match with the individual's capabilities, and a reasonable workload.

When people are struggling with a job for which they are not sufficiently qualified, it is difficult for them to feel confident or competent. When people are in an idle waiting period, which creates boredom, when they are so overworked that they don't have time to do anything well, or when they are uncertain about what is expected of them, then their motivation also drops. A workflow that is even in volume and that only somewhat exceeds present capabilities is the ideal (though many project managers who read this will view this ideal as the antithesis of their own experience).

Workflow planning is at least as critical in temporary systems as in permanent ones. In planning *Night Moves*, the producer had budgeted shooting time and costs with great precision. The tight schedule produced a continual sense of pressure, but people also derived a sense of satisfaction in meeting the schedule effectively day by day.

3. *The need for approval and appreciation*—Arthur Penn's sensitivity to, and responsiveness in working with, actors is unusual. Actors were pleased to know that he valued and appreciated both their technical and their personal abilities. His genuine yet discriminating approval and encouragement freed actors from anxiety about his acceptance of their work and released psychological energy which enabled them to go on performing as well or better, even when they were tired. Penn's ability to express his appreciation articulately and nonverbally was a key factor in creating an encouraging climate for the actors.

The ability to provide clear, realistic, positive feedback is unusual. In the business world, managers finding this difficult often tend to emphasize the negative. One manager we know said to a top subordinate at performance appraisal time, "I've given you an A on everything. You know what's good so let's talk about the bad," and then proceeded to do so for an hour. The absence of managerial approval can have several causes. Many managers are embarrassed at either giving or receiving praise. Some also find it hard to describe exactly what it is about a piece of work or a person that they value. In U.S. society there is also a semiconscious fear that the giving and receiving of verbal approval between men is somehow effeminate—much better to do it with a slap on the back.

Finally, there is the matter of organizational culture. In the film and theater world, people tend to express feelings more openly and spontaneously than elsewhere; that is their main task, and they have unusual skill in doing so. But the style that is usual in the acting world can sound effusive and insincere in a more austere technical or scientific setting. However, if expression of approval is to be an effective means of motivation, each manager has to find a language in which to phrase it; a language that sounds natural both to the organization and to him or her personally.

4. *Long-term career self-interest*—In the case of this film unit, Penn's reputation and past successes undoubtedly attracted people who hoped to learn and develop while working with him. They hoped to enhance their own professional reputation through both the high quality of work they expected to accomplish under his direction and their association with a film they hoped would be a commercial success.

Similarly, people who are looking for career growth and financial rewards in business organizations tend to be keenly aware of the effects of present performance on future assignments. Business people are likely to value tasks that contribute to their future development above tasks that offer only a repetition of past experience or a technical detour away from their main career. In order to create maximal fit between personal aspirations and task needs, managers must find time to ask people about their career plans and to listen to what they have to say about them.

Some managers are reluctant to do this because they fear that conversations about career goals will raise unrealistic hopes in their subordinates, or that during the conversation they will commit themselves to promises they cannot fulfill. But most subordinates are realistic enough to know that it is impossible to satisfy all their needs even most of the time.

Instead, they are likely to be motivated almost as much by the knowledge that their manager is making an effort to understand and take account of their interests, as they are by any actual opportunities for growth that managers offer them.

STIMULATING CREATIVITY

There is another aspect of motivation so important that we want to pay separate attention to it. Because of Penn's approach to film making, and his emphasis on the acting moment, his working relationships with actors were of crucial importance. He needed them to behave in ways that were spontaneous, authentic, original, and imaginative; to take risks by trying things they perhaps had never tried before; to be open to his suggestions and ideas; and to develop new ideas of their own and work with them. He was constantly open to the moment, not only abandoning his own preconceived ideas about how a line or scene should be played, but also actively helping actors shed their own preconceptions as well.

Susan Clark, the actress, commented: "Arthur maintains a two-way avenue of communication which must be kept open for suggestions and changes; the relationship is vital." Gene Hackman said: "Not only did he set everything up beautifully but he can think on his feet. He wings it as well as he plans it and maybe even a little better. That's his power. That's what's fresh in the film. Any moment, you may catch an idea. When an idea is new and infused with that thought energy, it tends to spark alive and all sorts of things can happen."

Penn's encouragement and enthusiasm both elicited and rewarded the actor's performances as well their trust in him. One particular technique contributed to this good working relationship. If Penn was dissatisfied, he would never give blatant negative feedback. Instead, making very small adjustments, he would keep asking his actors for something more: "This time maybe you could take a little more time" or "Let the hand go a little earlier." By encouraging his actors to adopt a different tone or attitude in their behavior rather than criticizing the whole performance and person, Penn avoided damaging the actor's sense of confidence and competence.

Another thing Penn did to avoid negative feedback was to refrain from interrupting a take once he had started it. His patience deliberately avoided the implication, "It's so bad that I don't want to see any more of it." The fact that even their unsuccessful efforts received respect was an important condition for risk taking in creative work.

By contrast, Penn was directive and relatively distant with the technical crews, from whom he demanded little spontaneous creativity. Because he needed to spend so much time with his actors, Penn collaborated little with the technical people themselves, leaving the responsibility for their technical effectiveness to the directors of photography, sound, and art work.

Penn's style of work—filming many versions of the same scene—made the technical workload particularly heavy. Sometimes the sheer pressure of work led the crews to feel that technical quality was being sacrificed. This mattered to them because their reputation depended on the opinion of studio heads who looked at the day-by-day screenings. Not all the technical personnel understood Penn's way of working. People who had mostly worked on films where planning and closure occurred in preproduction assumed at first that his openness to improvisation denoted uncertainty, that "he didn't know beforehand what he wanted to do," and that he "wasn't sure." When crew members did come to understand his style, they realized that the final choice about what the film was to contain would come in the postproduction phase, and felt excluded from the creative process.

Because of his priorities, Penn—consciously or unconsciously—varied the way in which he related to people. While he took time for actors to develop the spontaneous ideas and behavior which he needed, he also handled the stresses of time schedule and budget in a way which ensured that the production phase was completed on time.

LEADERSHIP STYLE

See "Three Directors' Approaches to Film Making" at the end of this article, where we describe major differences between the work styles of directors such as Alfred Hitchcock, Ingmar Bergman, and Arthur Penn. All three men produce fine films, but each has a different approach to the development of ideas and to the stage at which decisions are made and closure is reached.

Any temporary system has a timespan within which it must both generate the idea or design of its product, and then carry this through to a finished form. During this process there will be periods when the emphasis is on the production of ideas and alternatives, on improvisation, exploration, and experimentation. And there will be periods when ideas must be evaluated, decisions made, and movement accelerated toward closure of some kind.

Given the degree of precision and detailed planning that most scientific and engineering endeavors require, it seems unlikely that the spectrum of possible managerial styles would be as broad as the spectrum from Hitchcock to Penn, but some variation will undoubtedly exist.

A key element to a project's success will, therefore, be the manager's ability to distinguish between the "idea-generating" and "decision-making" periods as they occur and alternate in his organization; to determine how much overlap he wishes to encourage between them; and to find ways of relating to subordinates according to their engagement in either of these phases. The manager needs to orchestrate the two appropriately. For while being authoritarian when ideas are needed certainly kills creativity, being appreciative and acceptant when a major decision is needed can kill the whole project, or prevent it moving to a next vital stage on time.

It is our impression that most managers are trained to handle the management of the implementation phase better than the management of the "generative" phase. We have described how Penn worked to create a climate of acceptance and encouragement that freed creativity by reducing actors' anxiety about their work. Management of anxiety is an important part of a manager's role. He needs both to understand its negative effects and to avoid behavior which is likely to arouse it, as well as protect subordinates from external stresses which are likely to cause it.

It is possible for managers in business and industry to follow Penn's example, and many do so intuitively. But it is rarer for a manager to consider this process consciously, or to try to become aware of the different ways in which he needs to relate to different people, or to the same people at different times. The intensity of the director-actor relationship will not necessarily occur or be appropriate in all temporary systems. In some scientific or manufacturing environments, for instance, the same intensity might seem excessive. But there are equivalent behaviors in all organizations and cultures that communicate a basic acceptance of people and their ideas, and encourage them to produce more good ones.

All of this goes further to explain why a director's or manager's own personal behavior is a very important source of motivation in a temporary system. He or she can show personal appreciation and approval, or he can show neglect, apathy, or disapproval. He can motivate through personal attention and social contact. He can demotivate by separating himself from certain members of the organization— which may happen inevitably even though he would want it otherwise. He can increase or decrease the amount of creative participation that he invites from different people, and vary the intensity of his working relationship with them. All these are subtle, often nonverbal, interpersonal cues.

At the same time it is impossible for any manager to interact closely with a large group of people for a long period of time. In the film unit, the technical crew felt undervalued because the director's main attention was on the actors. There may be such groups in any temporary organization. One way to avoid such a problem is for the manager to identify those people who, for some reason, he will pay less attention to, and plan a complementary role for a subordinate who can provide the necessary recognition, appreciation, or encouragement.

Another approach a manager can use is to hire a subordinate whose personal style complements rather than coincides with his or her own. This goes against the grain of most people's natural tendency to hire others with the same characteristics and values as their own, but it does eliminate the strain of denying one's own limitations and attempting to play a "supermanager" role.

STRESS AND CONFLICT

How did people cope with the stresses caused by tight time and budget pressures, estrangement from familiar people and surroundings, and uncertainty about how good the film would be?

One important element in reducing stress was the norm of helpful collaboration that prevailed. This took the form of sensitivity to other people's feelings, and a willingness to provide interpersonal support. Usually this consisted of a symbolic gesture of some kind that could vary from a sympathetic look or a pat on the back, to doing an errand for someone, listening to a person's worries, or—in the case of an actress—cooking a Thanksgiving dinner for a group of people on location. Nurturant gestures of this kind were protective and reassuring. They gave people a sense that, to some small extent, others were willing to take care of them in a way that normally occurs more in personal life than at work. Such gestures were their usual source of caring and concern.

Symbolic support of this kind can also have considerable importance between a manager and a group of subordinates, as well as between individuals. For example, in one high-technology company, an over-burdened project team was told that the company president had called a meeting at a nearby hotel late on Friday afternoon, which everyone had to attend. They arrived, tired and dispirited, expecting a heavy chewing out over time-schedule delays. Instead, they found themselves at a surprise cocktail party, hearing the president say: "There's still a long way to go, but I want you to know we appreciate your efforts so far." Then he sent everyone home.

Penn dealt with stresses caused by interruption through unusually careful protection of the work areas. Gene Hackman explained the reason: "There's a funny kind of family atmosphere on a film that is generally created by the director. Many times that family balloon can be punctured quite readily by an outside influence. If you are working on a scene and you see out of the corner of your eye a foreign object, someone standing by the camera, I for one, get a little tight."

In the business and industrial world, geographic boundaries are less easily monitored, but there are other ways of protecting people's concentration on the task. For example, many disturbances tend to be caused by organizational or personal administrative problems. In some cases it may be worth appointing a support person who can buffer disturbances from the outside, and can service the team—for instance, someone who will follow up on a lost paycheck, an undelivered desk, a purchasing snarl-up, or a leaking roof above a drawing board.

It may even be worth having someone take care of minor personal needs too, such as making dental or hairdresser's appointments, cashing checks, or finding out whether a repaired car is ready for pickup. There is a common assumption that "personal" administrative problems should be taken care of by the individual, but all too often this can only be done during working hours. In the film unit the production secretaries provided such personal services. Penn worked under the notion that "anything which disturbs is a disturbance," and did not try to categorize distractions as "personal" or "official."

Another common source of stress in temporary groups is the conflict that occurs between people who must work closely together. One of the main thrusts of current organizational development work is the encouragement of conflict resolution by means of confrontation. However, time in a film unit—a marginal cost of $25,000 per day for *Night Moves*—is too valuable to spend on resolving difficulties in working relationships which will soon come to an end. Here a major professional convention of the film business protected the work. This unwritten law requires that no matter how tense, dissatisfied, or upset actors and director may be, they keep their complaints and conflicts off the set and out of formal working hours. In nonworking hours people dealt with stress in various ways. Some withdrew—to books, music, alcohol, or drugs. Some became more than usually gregarious.

One main source of potential stress and tension in every temporary—and permanent—system is rarely talked about. It is the personal behavior of the manager. For example, some managers look only for problems and faults in whatever their colleagues and subordinates tell them. As a result, subordinates may tend actively to avoid such a manager in order to protect themselves from the angry feelings which such critical behavior arouses.

Managers can do even very small things that contribute to or alleviate stress if they continually repeat them. For instance, if a team is somewhat slow in ending a coffee break, the director or manager can adopt an authoritarian tone of voice and yell his orders to "get back to work." Or he can stand up, point silently to his watch, and rely on his subordinates' sense of professionalism to motivate them to get moving. In the latter case, there is less chance that employees will experience the message as a reproach, and so less chance that the level of confidence and trust which they have in their manager will be reduced.

Because he was so acutely aware of the schedule, Penn was a hard taskmaster, asking people to work intensely for long hours. Gene Hackman described the way in which Penn could turn the time pressure he was under into increased work momentum for the actors: "He is a terrific manager. He keeps it rolling. There is a little part of his brain that is counting dollars. But when he tells you to keep it rolling, he tells you, 'good for your energy; let's keep it moving.' "

Most temporary systems share the stresses of the film unit the production film unit: uncertainty of outcome, intense time and budget pressures, long hours of work, and more than usual interdependence between fellow workers. In looking for ways to think about this aspect of their responsibilities, many managers, particularly scientists and engineers, naturally look to physical models stress. As a result they make the assumption that stress in human beings is akin to stress in materials; that everything will be fine as long as a certain limit of elasticity is not passed. But, unfortunately, stress in people is cumulative. The only way for a manager to be aware of how much and what kind of stress his people are experiencing is to monitor it—by asking them and listening to what they tell him.

The final stress that film and theater people manage well is the business of "letting go." The director or producer usually arranges some event that marks closure—such as a cast party. And in fact many managers do the same, using a party or dinner as an opportunity to make a final expression of appreciation, to plan a moment for their subordinates to celebrate and take pride in their achievements before moving on. People who manage this kind of ritual smoothly are at an advantage, but it does not come naturally to everyone. In this case the manager needs to find someone who will help or even do this for him; one's own boss is the first source of help. The process also has some importance to the manager of the project to which people are next assigned. For if management has provided some appropriate ending that gives subordinates a sense of closure on their last project, people will feel psychologically freer to commit themselves to the next task.

Rewards of Temporary Systems

A friend in the film world summed up the challenge of working in temporary systems for us: "Really the thing about temporary systems is that you have to be more interpersonally competent. People have to be able to accept bull and come back the next day and get on with the work just the same; live through crisis and stress and provide support for each other to get through it; and still keep the creative ideas coming, through it all."

In businesses—such as the film industry and the theater—where high levels of interpersonal sensitivity and expressiveness are necessary to complete the system's task most people are already interpersonally competent. They are trained to be. But in organizations where the task depends on a process of scientific rationality, interpersonal competence is not immediately and self-evidently necessary, and tends not to be highly valued. The skills needed to manage or be a member of a temporary system will not be in great supply, and may even be regarded as "counterculture."

The cultivation of higher levels of interpersonal skill in temporary systems, which do not have an intrinsic high value for them, is an area in which more research and experimentation is urgently needed. We have two reasons for saying this. One is, of course, related to the elimination of problems that prevent tasks being accomplished successfully. The other is related to the quality of human experience that can occur in a temporary organization.

Part of the excitement in making a film comes from the product. The creation of a film involves more drama and more opportunity for fantasy, for personal expressiveness and emotionality, than does the manufacture of, say, a refrigerator or a computer program. But some of the excitement comes from the organizational form itself. Temporary systems provide opportunities for intensity in work, and for closeness and commitment in working relationships which many, though not all, of us enjoy and value highly for limited periods of time. Because of these time and membership limits and the mutual commitment to a clear common goal, temporary systems have the potential for being more exciting places to work than permanent ones.

People who have participated in such systems often have a sense of having experienced their work life more fully and excitingly than in other settings. Not all the experience is necessarily good. Obviously it includes stress, frustration, and sometimes isolation. But because the goal is circumscribed and time-limited, it becomes possible for people to put out a greater effort to achieve it than is possible on a continuing basis. When the exertion of such effort is accomplished by achievement of the goal, by fruitful collaborative relationships with others, and by the appreciation of those who led the work, most people experience an important and positive sense of satisfaction.

Three Directors' Approaches to Film Making

FILM DIRECTORS VIEW the creative process in one of two ways: either as something they carefully work out in advance or as something they improvise as they go along. The form and content of the film can be more or less fixed in either of the three phases of preproduction, production, or postproduction. The director's strategic preference for which phase is most important is a function of his personal style.

Some directors prepare films as fully as possible in advance. They know exactly what they want: "It's all in their heads." They put it down on paper and have a completely detailed shooting script before the first shot is made. In this case, the conceptualization of the film occurs completely in the preproduction phase. Shooting and editing become a matter of carrying out predetermined instructions in order to construct something that faithfully represents what has already been imagined. Directors who use this approach in effect make all creative choices in preproduction and achieve a maximum amount of closure before shooting begins.

Alfred Hitchcock is a director who puts maximum emphasis on preproduction. He makes and fixes all his decisions in advance. In preproduction he works out a full shooting script and editing plan, leaving no opportunity for later changes as the result of creative collaboration with actors or editor. Often he is not even present during production. For Hitchcock, the exciting part of film making is in the planning. Hitchcock has said: "When I've gone through the script and created the picture on paper, for me the creative job is done, and the rest is just a bore."[1]

Other directors prefer to leave conceptualization open at least through the production phase. For them a crucial aspect of the creative process occurs in improvising and collaborating with actors and/or technicians to evolve the film—perhaps a collaboration which they repeat with some of the same people from film to film. For some directors the making of a film is a search. They do not know exactly what they will do, but in production they find it.

Ingmar Bergman also spends time on his scripts which he writes himself, and in planning his films. However, these efforts are simply the technical basis for the creative process that occurs in production as he works with the actors, and where he is always willing to make script and shooting changes. Bergman wants to capture the fresh, creative urge that occurs in acting of the highest caliber, which is characterized by a spontaneity that cannot be practiced in advance. Bergman once said about his search for the creative urge: "I believe it is precisely this which keeps me in films, holds me fascinated by the medium. The development and retention of a sudden burst of life. . . ."[2]

The range of a director's choice in the postproduction phase depends on his "heaviness" or power. The index which most defines the director's authority is the profitability of his last film. If it was a blockbuster he will have "final cut" authority on his next film. That is to say, no one will have the right to change his final edited version. If he does not have final cut authority, he probably will have the right to "preview cut" but the distributing organization will retain the right to make subsequent changes.

But only if the director has final cut power, as Arthur Penn does, can the finished film be the result of one man's vision. In such a case everyone has to defer to his creative conceptualization, which is one of the norms of the industry. Many people are anxious to work with directors who have this heavy-weight authority, for with it go power, respect, and charisma. Less meddling and much less compromise occur on such a film.

Directors who are able to defer final choices until the postproduction editing phase can do so by having a very high shooting ratio (the number of feet of film exposed during the production relative to the actual length of the final film); and a very high coverage (the number of the different ways in which a particular film is shot). They may take many different versions of a scene without reaching a final conclusion about the way in which they want the audience to experience it.

Arthur Penn's approach to film making is much closer to that of Bergman than to Hitchcock. In his judgment it is critical for the acting process to be one of immediacy and freshness, spontaneity and authenticity. His objective is to create an authentic happening which, in being photographed, will generate the film material. He wants to create this in as many forms as possible; to photograph it in as many ways as possible, leaving the choice of what will appear in the final film until the editing phase. This is both an exciting and taxing way to work, and the importance of his leadership style lies in the way he brings it about.

Notes

1. Francois Truffaut, *Hitchcock* (New York: Simon & Schuster, 1967).

2. Stig Bjorkman et al., *Bergman on Bergman* (New York: Simon & Schuster, 1974).

Originally published in March–April 1977
Reprint 77210

Author's note: We wish to express our warm thanks to Arthur Penn for encouraging this research, and for allowing us to describe this work.

What's Stifling the Creativity at CoolBurst?

SUZY WETLAUFER

Executive Summary

THIS FICTITIOUS CASE STUDY explores the challenges facing CoolBurst, a Miami-based fruit-juice company. For over a decade, CoolBurst had ruled the market in the Southeast. Why, then, are its annual revenues stuck at $30 million, and why have profits been stagnant for four years straight? CoolBurst's new CEO, Luisa Reboredo, knows that the company's survival—and her own—depend on the answers.

It doesn't help that Reboredo's teenage son, Alfonse, prefers the drinks of CoolBurst's biggest competitor, or that half a dozen start-ups have recently joined the competitive fray. Nor does it help that Reboredo has succeeded former utilitarian CEO Garth LaRoue. While LaRoue had undeniably made CoolBurst into the well-oiled machine it was, he'd also been stubborn about enforcing a culture of tradition, self-discipline, and respect for authority—a culture so staid and polite, it left little room for employees to be creative. LaRoue, for instance, had almost fired two of CoolBurst's most creative employees for inventing four new drinks without his permission.

Sam Jenkins, one of those employees, had been so angered by the incident that he left the company to work for CoolBurst's largest competitor. Most of his colleagues had been overjoyed to see him go—he was a troublemaker, they said. But Reboredo understood the company's loss, and she knew that Jenkins's creative spark was now what CoolBurst needed most to save itself.

How can Reboredo encourage her employees to start thinking the way Jenkins did? And how can she nurture any creative individuals who may join the company in the future? Five experts give advice on how Reboredo can fire up CoolBurst's creative juices.

LUISA REBOREDO HAD NEVER been one to count her hours in the office, let alone take all the vacation days she had accumulated in her 15 years with Cool-Burst, a Miami-based fruit-juice company. Now, as the newly appointed CEO, she seemed to live at work. The job exhilarated her, and she had big plans for the company's future—if she could just get performance on track first.

It took a great deal of pleading, therefore, for Reboredo's 18-year-old son, Alfonse, to get her to attend Miami's popular outdoor art festival with him one Saturday in May. She had regularly been working weekends, using the time to pore over CoolBurst's books in an effort to figure out why annual revenues were stuck at $30 million and why profits hadn't risen for four years straight.

Finally, the two struck a deal: Luisa would attend the art festival in the morning and spend the rest of the day at the office.

They arrived at 10, and already the sun was baking the festival grounds. Alfonse, almost a full foot taller than Luisa and a basketball star at Southwest Miami High, put his arm around his mother. "Mom, this is great—you've got to get out more often," he practically sang. "You're missing the action stuck inside that office."

Luisa sighed. Raising Alfonse by herself hadn't been easy, and now that she had reached the top of her career and could comfortably afford his college tuition, the last thing she wanted was to have the company she'd helped to build collapse beneath her. Just the thought of CoolBurst's stagnant performance suddenly made her tense. Why was it, she wondered, that CoolBurst wasn't growing anymore? For over a decade, it had been the most successful juice maker in the Southeast. Practically every school in Florida, Georgia, Alabama, and South Carolina had a CoolBurst vending machine in its cafeteria, and thousands of restaurants listed CoolBurst's apple, grape, and cranberry drinks by brand name on their menus. In fact, CoolBurst had grown so steadily over the years that its parent company, a Chicago-based conglomerate, rarely interfered with operations. Lately, however, Luisa had been receiving weekly phone calls from the higher-ups in Chicago inquiring about budget projections, expenses, and personnel changes.

"Mom, stop thinking about work!" Alfonse shouted, interrupting Luisa's thoughts. "You should see the expression on your face!"

Luisa tried to smile but shrugged instead. "I'm sorry, Alfonse," she said. "Let's look around."

Her son readily agreed, steering her toward a row of paintings by a local artist they both liked. Then Alfonse stopped for a moment. "Wait a second, Mom," he said, "let me grab a drink first. I'm burning up."

Alfonse dashed over to a man selling drinks from a cart a few yards away. The cart was topped by a large red umbrella emblazoned with the words Destroy Your Thirst! Drink a Thirst Smasher. A moment later, he was back, unscrewing the cap of a red glass bottle shaped like a rocket.

"Alfonse!" Luisa practically gasped. "How could you?"

"How could I what?" Alfonse replied, somewhat irritated. "I couldn't get a CoolBurst around here if I tried, Mom. I suppose I could sprint over to the high school, but that wouldn't exactly be convenient.

"Besides," Alfonse added, "everyone knows Cool-Burst is for kids. These Thirst Smashers are something new. Get a load of this flavor—Mango Tango. It tastes fabulous."

Luisa cringed—she knew all about Mango Tango. In fact, the flavor had been invented in CoolBurst's own labs, a collaboration between chief scientist Carol Velez and CoolBurst's then marketing director, Sam Jenkins. The two had concocted Mango Tango and four other exotic drinks on the sly about a year earlier. But when they presented them to the company's then CEO, Garth LaRoue, he had been so angry about their unauthorized use of time that he had practically fired them both. Velez hadn't had her heart in her job since. And Jenkins had left CoolBurst shortly thereafter to join Thirst Smashers, one of a half dozen start-ups that had recently begun venturing into the drink business in the Southeast. To Luisa, it felt as if every month a new company joined the competitive fray, each one coming from a different angle. Thirst Smashers was parking its drink carts on every corner. Drink-Ups, another new player, was selling carbonated juice drinks and advertising like mad on the radio with a jingle even she couldn't get out of her head.

But so far, Luisa reminded herself, none of the start-ups had put a noticeable dent in CoolBurst's market share in schools and restaurants. The reason, she figured, was the company's efficient set of systems, in both the factory and the field. CoolBurst's purchasing agents and plant operations were located in Atlanta, where managers worked to make a high-quality product as inexpensively as possible. The company's salespeople were all over the Southeast, developing close relationships with their customers. An advanced—and pricey—information technology system, which CoolBurst had installed in 1990, allowed salespeople in the field to place orders, which were filled swiftly by a fleet of CoolBurst drivers. And finally, the company's labs were located at headquarters, where Velez and a small staff focused on improving the flavors of CoolBurst's products and the efficiency of the company's factory processes.

CoolBurst is like a well-oiled machine, Luisa told herself: not many bells and whistles to what we do, but we do it well. Perhaps that was why it caused such a scandal when Velez and Jenkins got together to invent Mango Tango and the other new flavors. Everyone in the company was sick and tired of the way Jenkins was trying to

change things. Most employees considered him a troublemaker—a transplanted New Yorker and business
school graduate who did nothing but harangue people to
"think outside the box."

"What box is he talking about?" was the refrain from
most of CoolBurst's 200 employees, who were predominantly native Miamians who had joined the company
after high school or college. CoolBurst had been an independent company until 1975, and it still retained much
of its old organizational culture, which reflected the traditional, family-oriented background of its Cuban-born
founder.

Employees were loyal and conservative in both mind
and manner. The company's dress code was formal, even
in Miami's warm climate, and employees treated one
another with a politeness that seemed like a throwback
to the 1950s. But as old-fashioned as it seemed, that
politeness was an aspect of CoolBurst's culture that
employees valued highly. No one at CoolBurst argued.
No one swore. No one complained that the company's
offices were small and nondescript. No one ever
answered the phone in any way other than the expected
"Thank you for calling CoolBurst. How may I be of service?" The company was a calm and civilized place to
work in the midst of a changing, chaotic world.

It's no wonder, then, Luisa thought, that Sam Jenkins
rubbed a lot of people the wrong way: he was always
confronting colleagues about their assumptions and
ways of doing business. His favorite phrase was "Everyone's entitled to my opinion." And he seemed to delight
in challenging rules and norms around the office. He
often arrived late to work, left early, and blared rock-
and-roll music from his computer's CD-ROM drive.
Some days, when he left at lunchtime, he would tape a

note to his door that read, "Gone to the movies to get my creative juices flowing. Ha!" Even his office space seemed to challenge the status quo. The walls were covered with large, haunting photographs he had taken while traveling through Africa and India, and several fanciful "dream catchers" hung from the ceiling. When the phone rang, Jenkins always answered, "Yeah?"

Worse, his behavior had a negative effect on the productivity of other employees. When Jenkins left early, other people followed. If the director of marketing worked half days, they figured, why couldn't they? As a result, the phones in customer service often went unanswered.

Jenkins's work habits seemed to suit him: despite his odd hours, he always got a lot done. But Luisa—and many others in top management—had noticed that allowing other employees this freedom didn't seem to do much for the overall output of the company.

Luisa liked Jenkins. She knew he had passed up high-paying offers in consulting and on Wall Street to take the job at CoolBurst because, as he put it, he loved business "in the trenches." She also knew that, soon after starting at CoolBurst, Jenkins had quickly grown worried about the company. He told everyone who would listen that CoolBurst's past success had been a simple matter of being in the right place at the right time—and a fortuitous lack of competition. "The bubble is going to burst one of these days," he kept repeating. CoolBurst had to innovate, he warned—or it would evaporate.

Jenkins wanted to lead the charge. First, he started working on the director of distribution, Roger Blatt. Why was it, he asked, that CoolBurst was sold only in school vending machines and in restaurants? What about opening up new channels? How about handing out CoolBursts to everyone who stepped off a plane at Miami International Airport? Blatt nearly roared when he heard that suggestion. There were a hundred reasons why that couldn't be done. For one, the airport had extremely tight security regulations. And where would the drivers park? How could they possibly get the juice to the gates? And what about keeping it cold? Finance certainly wouldn't approve the idea anyway.

Blatt's final words on the matter were strong: "If it ain't broke, don't fix it."

For a while after his run-in with distribution, Jenkins restricted his creativity campaign to his own territory. His first idea was to get CoolBurst—or maybe even its corporate parent—to cough up some money for advertising. Sure, CoolBurst had advertised in the past, but minimally, and never on TV. In fact, all advertising had been designed in-house and usually consisted of point-of-purchase posters. Jenkins had a different plan in mind. CoolBurst needed fresh minds from outside the company to help create a new vision of the brand. After making his case for three months, he was given a modest budget. He immediately hired a New York firm well known for its jazzy TV commercials.

But the agency didn't last long at CoolBurst. In their first meeting with CoolBurst's management team, the account executives launched into what they called a "creativity-enhancement exercise." After dimming the lights, they urged the CoolBurst managers to close their eyes and imagine themselves on a desert island, dying of thirst. "Suddenly, an angel arrives and offers you the drink of your dreams. Let your imagi-

Jenkins and Velez presented their new drinks to LaRoue, only to be shouted out of his office.

nation go—you can have anything you want—no constraints," incanted one ad executive. "Let yourself
fantasize."

"That's enough!" snapped LaRoue, who was still CEO
at the time. "I'm all for new ideas around here, but these
kinds of mind games are a waste of time. Either you're
born creative or you're not. Fantasizing about an angel
isn't going to do us a bit of good. We all should be back
at our desks working."

LaRoue's comments hadn't surprised Luisa. He was
nearing 65 and had been at CoolBurst his entire career,
starting as a stock boy in the factory. He valued tradition, just as he valued self-discipline and respect for
authority. He had quickly come to distrust Jenkins, and,
after the incident with the advertising agency, he had
strongly urged Luisa to get rid of him.

Even if she had wanted to, Luisa didn't have the
chance. A few days later, Jenkins and Velez presented
their four new drinks to
LaRoue, only to be shouted out
of his office. When Luisa found
Velez back in the lab later, she
was dejectedly pouring the
prototypes down the drain.

*"We've got one
creative person here,
and he makes
everyone nervous."*

Luisa stopped her before she emptied the Mango
Tango, and took a taste. It was delicious, and she told
her so.

"It doesn't make any difference that it's delicious,"
said Velez. "You can't do anything different in this company. Everyone gets hysterical."

"Well, I won't get hysterical," Luisa said, "and I may
soon have the final say as the new CEO."

"Forget it," said Velez. "That's not what CoolBurst is
about. We're not a creative company. We're just a little

juice company that knows how to do one thing well—
make plain old juice and deliver it to plain old schools
and restaurants." She looked Luisa straight in the eye.
"We've got one creative person here, and he makes
everyone nervous. Even if you told everyone it was okay
to be creative like Sam Jenkins, no one would know what
to do. How do you make a bunch of people who are
happy doing the same old thing come up with new
ideas? It's just not the CoolBurst way."

Velez's assertion didn't make Luisa happy, but it
couldn't be denied. CoolBurst wasn't a creative place,
and it didn't attract creative people—with the exception
of Jenkins and Velez. And when it did find that rare creative person who wanted to make a difference, management didn't know what to do with him—apart from
forcing him out the door.

As Luisa stood outside in the blazing sun with
Alfonse—who was polishing off his Mango Tango Thirst
Smasher—she couldn't stop thinking about Velez's
assessment of CoolBurst. Was the company really a lost
cause when it came to the issue of creativity? Were its
employees really as stolid as Velez thought they were?
And was there some way to get everyone—from distribution to manufacturing—to think of new and exciting
ways to revitalize CoolBurst's product line and way of
doing business?

Was there a way, Luisa wondered, to make CoolBurst
a more welcoming, nurturing place for creative individuals like Jenkins? Sure, some of his ideas were off the wall;
Luisa smiled to herself as she remembered his plan to
have thousands of bottles of CoolBurst wash up on the
Miami beaches during spring break. But others, such as
exotic new flavors, were terrific.

"Hey, Mom, you're still thinking about work!" Alfonse broke into Luisa's thoughts once more. "Let's have some fun. Let me buy you a Mango Tango!"

How Can Reboredo Foster Creativity in Her Current Employees and Nurture Creative Individuals Who Join the Company in the Future?

Five experts examine the issue of building creativity in the workplace.

PAUL BARKER *has been at Hallmark Cards for 18 years and is general manager of its Everyday Cards division in Kansas City, Missouri. He has managed a variety of departments, such as the greeting card studios, the photography group, the digital studio, and the specialty-gift design department. He also has led the development and marketing of Everyday Cards' product programs.*

At least Luisa Reboredo wants CoolBurst to become a creatively competitive company. The first step toward successful change is having an engaged CEO who truly believes in the company's vision. But right now, she seems to think that achieving success has to be a radical, wrenching experience. It doesn't. She also seems to think that all change is big change. It isn't. CoolBurst has creative thinkers in its ranks right now, and Reboredo can draw on that creativity without causing a corporate crisis. Sam Jenkins was too much too fast for a company that is accustomed to a quiet cultural evolution. The trick is to encourage meaningful change gradually so that the troops that made the company so successful in the past are not threatened but engaged.

How can she do it? The first step is to change her own mind-set. Reboredo must stop thinking about Cool-Burst as if it were frozen in time, relying solely on its past successes. Sure, the company has done things a certain way for many years—and it has done them extremely well. But yesterday's and today's experiences are part of a much longer journey. Reboredo must come to understand that she can—and should—use the past and the present to build the future. CoolBurst has a heritage and a culture to be proud of, and she shouldn't discount that. But there's no need for her to remain mired in them, either.

Creativity at CoolBurst should not be confined to the marketing and product development departments.

Reboredo must also revisit her perception of what creativity is and where it resides. Creativity at CoolBurst need not and should not be confined to the marketing and product development departments. Her people in inventory and operations need to be creative as well, as do her administrative assistants. She needs to tap into every employee's creativity if the business is ever going to live up to its potential.

With those things in mind, Reboredo should start thinking about long-term goals. What is her definition of victory? Where does she want the company to be in three years? In five? A good leader will develop new long-term goals even as the old long-term action plans are being played out. The trick is to understand how past successes can be linked to a future vision.

Then she must prepare a new action plan. If Reboredo goes to her employees with a message about change but with few specifics to back it up, she will scare them and fail to get them committed to molding a new future for the company. What are some specific, relatively safe ideas that her people will be comfortable with? What particular areas should Reboredo target first? Flavors? Distribution? She should encourage a step-by-step approach and be able to say to her staff, "If we start to measure ourselves against the alternatives available to our customers, and if we begin to look at this particular part of the product differently, what can we accomplish?" She can't just flip a switch and say, "We're there."

Once she has a well-defined plan, it's time for Reboredo to talk with her employees—through personal meetings, memos, E-mail—employing any and all modes of communication used by the company. Her general message should be something to the effect of, "We've done well, and we can continue to do well as our industry evolves. Now let's start adding a little bit more into our mix."

The beauty of Reboredo's situation is that her current employees already have the knowledge they need to act on new ideas. *Reboredo should ask employees to consider how competitors view CoolBurst.* They understand what procedures work well, and they'll know how to blend in new approaches. They'll also know what kind of change won't work given their current capabilities, so they'll be able to assess degrees of risk from the get-go.

As for getting her employees to think creatively, there are a number of things Reboredo can try. One exercise that can be particularly useful in identifying opportunities for improvement and change is to ask employees to think about how competitors view the company. Where is CoolBurst vulnerable? What might competitors do to take advantage of any weakness?

Another idea is to get her employees out of the office for a day or for a few days—under the right circumstances and with the proper follow-up actions. For example, they might attend a sporting event where competitors' drinks are sold, then return to the office and meet to discuss important findings. Time spent out of the office may appear to be wasted, but if it is spent thinking about the company and the product, it can yield great results. Jenkins wasn't wrong to leave work early and go to the movies, but the other employees began to copy his behavior without truly understanding his reasons. Jenkins knew how to use experiences outside the company to foster his own creativity. Those experiences helped him figure out what motivated different kinds of people and enabled him to identify what sorts of things influenced their tastes and lifestyles. More important, he knew how to bring those insights back into the company. Reboredo needs to get her people to think as freely as Jenkins did; she needs to get them out of the office and help them use those external experiences to energize the company.

At Hallmark, we send some of our most creative people to places that on the surface appear to have nothing to do with greeting cards. For example, we'll send groups of our writers and artists on trips to New Mexico or Wyoming. When these people witness a sunrise over an incredible mountain landscape, they tend to get a heightened appreciation for emotional experiences. While in the presence of such breathtaking beauty, they are often able to tap into creativity they were unable to tap into back at the office. And by focusing that creative energy on the product, they can find new ways to express almost any emotion. They even can find new ways to wish someone a happy birthday.

We do it with cards, but there's no reason Reboredo can't use similar activities to help her employees develop new ways to create, package, distribute, and market her company's juice drinks. Mango Tango may have taken the lead, but CoolBurst is by no means out of the race.

TERESA M. AMABILE *is the M.B.A. Class of 1954 Professor of Business Administration at the Harvard Business School in Boston, Massachusetts. Her 20 years of research, summarized in* Creativity in Context *(Westview Press, 1996), have focused on how the work environment can affect motivation, creativity, and innovation.*

Jenkins may have been a pain in the neck, but he was right about at least one thing: when faced with increasing competition, a company must innovate or evaporate. Part of Reboredo's job as CEO is to convince the Roger Blatts of the company that even if their way of doing business "ain't broke," that doesn't mean it's working. CoolBurst's competitors are already winning the hearts, minds, and taste buds of a primary customer base—kids like Reboredo's son, Alfonse. If CoolBurst continues to do business as usual, it most likely won't be doing business for very long.

What can Reboredo do? To begin, I'd encourage her to change her own thinking about creativity. Her predecessor, Garth LaRoue, sounded a bit extreme when he said, "Either you're born creative or you're not," but he was expressing an all-too-common belief—and one that Reboredo shares, whether or not she realizes it. For example, she says that CoolBurst doesn't attract creative people. But all people with normal human capacities can be creative, meaning

Most of the creative work done in the world gets done by ordinary people.

they can produce ideas that are both novel and useful. And all areas of human endeavor—not just product development and advertising—are possible arenas for creative thinking. Certainly, not everyone will produce genius-level breakthroughs. But most of the creative work that gets done in the world gets done by ordinary people who continually try to approach their work with a fresh perspective—people who will never be famous. I agree that Reboredo should bring in some new blood. But if she thinks that the best you can do is to find creative people and then sit back and wait for them to create, she has failed to realize her own power to make a difference.

Consider the following: In our research, my students and I have found that people are most creative when they have three things: expertise, creative-thinking skills, and intrinsic motivation. By *expertise,* I mean knowledge, experience, skills, and talents in the areas in which they are working. Reboredo should try to think broadly about the kinds of expertise that might be useful for her company in the future. By *creative-thinking skills,* I mean ways of coming up with fresh perspectives on problems and ways of approaching work from new angles. These skills can be developed, even though I share LaRoue's skepticism about quick-fix creative-thinking exercises. Research, however, supports the idea that people can learn to think in more original ways through careful training in creative problem-solving techniques.

By *intrinsic motivation,* I mean a combination of one's own internal drive and the environmental factors that support it. Reboredo must find people who are passionately interested in taking on the challenges of Cool-Burst's business—people such as Velez and Jenkins, who had the drive, even though the company killed it. Reboredo must try to create an atmosphere that will allow creativity to bubble up freely. She might, for example, think about setting aside some resources specifically for innovative projects and allotting time for experimentation. The famous "15% Rule" at 3M, whereby scientists are expected to devote 15% of their time to invention, is not a bad guide. She might also think about creating work groups composed of people with diverse sets of skills and perspectives—anything that stimulates interest and engages employees in creative pursuits.

Also, although there is little evidence that the physical environment significantly affects creativity, I would encourage Reboredo to try toning down the formal atmosphere at CoolBurst. A slight change in the dress code or in the office setup could signal to both old-timers and newcomers that it is now acceptable to do things differently.

Above all, she should try to ensure that the company's managers—including herself—do not display an attitude that implies a knee-jerk protection of the status quo. Through open communication, she and other members of her team can help employees orient the company toward industry leadership by encouraging them to look consistently for new and better ways of doing business. Reboredo must try to step back and understand how her behavior—and that of other senior managers—are seen by her employees. And the next time someone creates a delicious new flavor, she should be sure to celebrate the breakthrough by walking it through every department.

Similarly, if someone suggests a new way to look at distribution systems, she must be sure that people make a serious attempt to see if the idea can work.

My suggestions imply a good deal of newfound freedom for CoolBurst's employees. How much is enough? Achieving the right balance between freedom and control is probably the most difficult task Reboredo faces in trying to foster creativity. Although Jenkins's unusual hours may have helped his creative productivity, such flexible schedules can cause trouble if no one is watching the store. Reboredo must try to establish a culture in which everyone knows what the goals are and everyone feels personally committed to meeting them. That way, even freedom has direction. And she should consider changing the performance-review and reward system to reflect the company's new culture.

People should be talking about their work within and across levels. They need to understand that CoolBurst is a place where great work is equitably recognized and generously rewarded. They shouldn't be looking over their shoulders, waiting for that review in which they are confronted with their mistakes. Reboredo must want people to work hard because they are challenged by difficult, interesting problems that they care about, not because they are pushing against arbitrary deadlines or because managers have dangled a carrot in front of them to make them behave a certain way.

Reboredo seems to realize that there are different ways of thinking about creativity and that there may be ways of fostering it within the company. She should trust her instincts. She knows the business, and Cool-Burst has a solid foundation on which to build. She is in a good position to start taking some risks—and, in the process, to start making mistakes from which she can extract some failure value. She shouldn't be afraid to take those risks; it's the only way to regain the lead her company once enjoyed. (For an in-depth discussion of Amabile's ideas, see "How to Kill Creativity" at the beginning of this book.)

MANFRED F.R. KETS DE VRIES *is the Clinical Professor of Management and Leadership and the Raoul de Vitry d'Avaucourt Professor in Human Resource Management at INSEAD in Fontainebleau, France. He also is a psychoanalyst.*

Poor Reboredo! She is faced with a challenge that she is barely aware of. As her son so accurately points out, she has been missing all the action. Ironically, if she had spent less time in her office and more time with her son and his friends (who constitute an important customer base with which she is remarkably unfamiliar), she might have realized sooner the need for a new image and more exciting products. There is a great difference between working hard and working smart!

What Reboredo needs to do to save the company—and make no mistake, it is in danger of collapse—is to dramatize CoolBurst's precarious situation in the market. She must make her employees aware that competitors pose a real threat to CoolBurst's stability. And she must do away with the current corporate culture of command, compartmentalization, and control. Such a climate only stifles creativity and innovation. She must create an environment in which there is what psychoanalysts call transitional space—in other words, where there is room for people to play. For creativity to flower, rules and regulations should be minimized.

Reboredo must become the kind of leader who envisions, empowers, and energizes. That is, she must question the status quo, provide a new focus, and encourage commitment and motivation. She needs to allow her employees to experiment and make mistakes; moreover, she needs to ensure that they are willing to take risks.

Is she up to the challenge? For the moment and for the purposes of a best-case scenario, let's give her the benefit of the doubt. Perhaps her own natural creativity had been stifled by her predecessor, and now, as the new CEO, Reboredo will be in a position to see and act differently. She may become courageous enough to follow her own impulses and shrug off her old control-oriented management style. If that is the case, she might even be able to forge a new competitive and creative spirit out of the pride her employees take in their past achievements. That is, she could use her employees' tradition of loyalty to the company as a lever to rally the troops.

Wouldn't it be nice if Reboredo were to have a chance encounter with Jenkins at the art festival? Getting together over piña coladas and reminiscing about old times, how things could have been different, might be just the stimulus she needs to get moving. Perhaps she would ask Jenkins to come back to CoolBurst. Having him back in the company would be symbolic of a change in the tide. Perhaps it would start a trend toward hiring the kind of people needed to revitalize CoolBurst—and toward prompting the people inside to think and act more creatively.

The newly charged Reboredo might also take the initiative to reconfirm her mandate with CoolBurst's corporate parent. If she were to find out exactly what the senior managers in Chicago thought of the Miami operation, she would be in a stronger position still.

Unfortunately, that best-case scenario is probably not the most likely. In fact, my sense is that Reboredo simply does not have the leadership qualities to set the necessary change process in motion. She seems much like one of CoolBurst's products—a loyal soldier without much flair or passion. And, as things stand, there does not seem to be enough pain in the system to force her to change. The company's lackluster performance and the increasing pressure from the parent company have not motivated Reboredo and most of her colleagues to challenge the status quo. And consider her track record: What is most disturbing about the Mango Tango incident is that Reboredo tasted the new product and liked it but failed to do anything about it. She made no effort to rally support for the new flavor, to build alliances, or to convince the CEO of the product's value. Instead, she preferred not to rock the boat. Given that, how can we be confident that she can be an effective catalyst for change?

I suspect I'm not alone in my assessment of Reboredo's performance and potential. The senior managers at CoolBurst's parent company are probably thinking the same thing. Indeed, the Chicago-based conglomerate does not seem to be the paragon of patience. Its managers are quite frustrated—and they have every reason to be. In which case, Reboredo may soon have the opportunity to spend lots of quality time with her son.

Most likely, the senior managers in Chicago have already reached the conclusion that Reboredo must be replaced. If they haven't, I would recommend that they do so. It has been said that chaos breeds life while order breeds habit. My sense is that only an outsider, preferably one familiar with the industry, can stir things up at CoolBurst—enough to breathe life back into the operation.

Of course, if they do replace Reboredo, she will not be the only person to leave. The new corporate culture will surely not suit everyone. It is possible that after so many years of socialization centered around rules and regulations, few people at CoolBurst still have a creative spark. After all, a climate of experimentation requires the presence of people who do not have to be prodded to do things, individuals with a high tolerance for ambiguity who are eager to learn and adapt. Can that latent spark still be fanned into a flame?

For the sake of CoolBurst's current employees—who do have a good deal to be proud of—I hope so. In economic theory, Gresham's law states that bad money drives out good money. Similarly, we can postulate a law of creativity whereby noncreative people are bound to drive out creative people—or vice versa. There can be no compromise if CoolBurst is to turn itself around and meet its new challenges successfully. It may be too late for Reboredo, but with the right leader, CoolBurst might rise to the occasion.

GARETH JONES *is the British Telecom Professor of Organisation Development at Henley Management College in Henley-on-Thames, England, and a visiting professor of organizational behavior at INSEAD in Fontainebleau, France. Prior to this appointment, he was senior vice president of human resources at Polygram International in London.*

ELSPETH MCFADZEAN *is a member of the information management faculty at Henley Management College. She also is on the board of directors at TeamTalk Consulting, a company based in Milton Keynes, England, that specializes in group facilitation and creative teamwork.*

It's clear that Reboredo must help unleash the creativity of her employees. But she should try not to become a "slash-and-burn" manager who on the way to the future ignores or puts down the company's past. That kind of behavior will only discourage her employees and stifle their creativity. Instead, she must identify CoolBurst's existing strengths and attempt to build on them. She should consider that she already has high-quality, low-cost manufacturing in place and that her salespeople and delivery systems are responsive to customers' needs. She should celebrate those great achievements with her employees and then move on. Creativity at CoolBurst should grow out of a sense of accomplishment.

How can she move forward? First, there are several things she should do quickly:

- Promote Velez—give her a fancy title and real scope in which to innovate. That will convince Velez that Reboredo means business. Velez, it must be remembered, was at least half of Mango Tango—and we think she still has a great deal of potential.

- Start a suggestion scheme—a simple box, perhaps. Many successful Japanese organizations use such simple methods to great effect. It might jump-start CoolBurst as well.

- Listen to her son! Reboredo does spend too much time at the office, and she is too close to the issues to see anything clearly. Perhaps she is a bigger part of the problem than she realizes. The fresh air seems to have done her good—she should take in a little more.

More broadly, Reboredo needs to think about ways to put the entire company on a new, creative track. We suggest that she do the following:

Encourage employees to take more risks. Reboredo must keep in mind, however, that employees will do so only if they believe that they work in a nonthreatening and supportive environment. Employees who face censorship and ridicule or who feel that they are at risk of losing their jobs are less likely to propose new ideas. Reboredo might consider establishing a system of collaboration that could be used by all the company's problem-solving groups and think tanks—a system in which team members would suggest new ideas anonymously and then develop the best ideas further with the group. That would facilitate consensus and reduce people's fear of risk.

Use creative problem-solving techniques, which can help groups and individuals view any situation from a different perspective. Reboredo must be careful, however, and remember what happened when the representatives from Jenkins's New York agency led their creativity-enhancement exercise. Advanced paradigm-breaking techniques, such as the *wishful thinking* exercise they tried to use, can be too much for people who are new to such things—too much because they may require a great deal of patience in trying to generate practical solutions. Reboredo would be better off starting with a paradigm-preserving technique, such as *brainwriting*, in which group members write down their ideas on paper and then have a facilitator share them with the group. This technique is particularly effective because it maintains anonymity and in doing so encourages equal participation. Reboredo then might consider moving on to a paradigm-stretching technique, such as *object stimulation*, in which group members come up with a list of objects unrelated to the problem at hand. Each individual in the group then chooses an object—perhaps a gardening tool or an animal—and describes it in detail. Such an exercise can

Any procedure in place simply because "that's the way it's always been done" must be challenged.

be more effective than a beginner exercise because it trains participants to look at a problem—as they would look at an object—from many angles.

Encourage employees to challenge their own perceptions of CoolBurst's products and processes. Employees should especially challenge any procedure that seems to be in place simply because "that's the way it has always been done." Reboredo might try forming a creative problem-solving team that includes employees from different functional areas in the company and from different levels. She might also think about hiring a trained facilitator to help. Such teams are effective because they tackle issues from so many different viewpoints and draw upon so many different skills and experiences.

Think positively. That may sound trite, but it's valid. Reboredo needs to encourage her employees to think positively when they are presented with new ideas. She needs to consider what might have happened had LaRoue taken Jenkins's suggestion to open up new distribution channels. What if CoolBurst's managers had tried to figure out a way to make the idea work? Blocking new ideas (no matter how silly they may seem) only discourages people. In the process of exploring Jenkins's idea, those managers might have come up with a plausible new distribution scheme. She should hold off on critical examination and risk assessment—there will be plenty of time for that later in the process.

Encourage "visioning." Reboredo should invite her employees to think about where they would like the company—or their department—to be in five years. Then she should encourage them to develop a plan for how to get there.

Employ rebels. Reboredo must hire people who are unlike most of those already at the company. These new hires will at first see CoolBurst differently than any of her current employees. She should try to learn from their perspectives and try not to let them sink into the existing culture. She needs to channel their ideas positively and appropriately.

Allow time for pet projects. Reboredo should consider setting aside time for employees to pursue their own work-related interests. The company will benefit tremendously, even if only a few new ideas come to fruition.

Ensure senior managers' support. This is a critical point. Often managers say they are supportive but don't behave as though they are. Senior managers must provide sufficient resources and training if any of Reboredo's efforts are to succeed. And each and every manager must be committed to the program—even Blatt. Perhaps Reboredo should consider sending him to a creativity seminar so that he can experience firsthand the powerful nature of innovative thinking.

We're confident about CoolBurst's future if Reboredo makes a start on this program. One last thought: liberating creativity is a continual process—not a one-shot deal!

Originally published in September–October 1997
Reprint 97511

Harvard Business Review's *cases present common managerial dilemmas and offer concrete solutions from experts. As written, they are hypothetical, and the names used are fictitious.*

The Discipline of Innovation

PETER F. DRUCKER

Executive Summary

SOME INNOVATIONS SPRING from a flash of genius. But as Peter Drucker points out, most result from a conscious, purposeful search for opportunities. For managers seeking innovation, engaging in disciplined work is more important than having an entrepreneurial personality.

Writing originally in the May–June 1985 issue, Drucker describes the major sources of opportunities for innovation. Within a company or industry, opportunities can be found in unexpected occurrences, incongruities of various kinds, process needs, or changes in an industry or market. Outside a company, opportunities arise from demographic changes, changes in perception, or new knowledge. These seven sources overlap, and the potential for innovation may well lie in more than one area at a time.

143

Innovations based on new knowledge, of course, tend to have the greatest effect on the marketplace. But it often takes decades before the ideas are translated into actual products, processes, or services. The other sources of innovation are easier and simpler to handle, yet they still require managers to look beyond established practices.

Drucker emphasizes that in seeking opportunities, innovators need to look for simple, focused solutions to real problems. The greatest praise an innovation can receive is for people to say "This is obvious!" Grandiose ideas designed to revolutionize an industry rarely work.

Innovation, like any other endeavor, takes talent, ingenuity, and knowledge. But Drucker cautions that if diligence, persistence, and commitment are lacking, companies are unlikely to succeed at the business of innovation.

Despite much discussion these days of the "entrepreneurial personality," few of the entrepreneurs with whom I have worked during the last 30 years had such personalities. But I have known many people—salespeople, surgeons, journalists, scholars, even musicians—who did have them without being the least bit "entrepreneurial." What all the successful entrepreneurs I have met have in common is not a certain kind of personality but a commitment to the systematic practice of innovation.

Innovation is the specific function of entrepreneurship, whether in an existing business, a public service institution, or a new venture started by a lone individual in the family kitchen. It is the means by which the entrepreneur either creates new wealth-producing resources or endows existing resources with enhanced potential for creating wealth.

Today, much confusion exists about the proper definition of *entrepreneurship*. Some observers use the term to refer to all small businesses; others, to all new businesses. In practice, however, a great many well-established businesses engage in highly successful entrepreneurship. The term, then, refers not to an enterprise's size or age but to a certain kind of activity. At the heart of that activity is innovation: the effort to create purposeful, focused change in an enterprise's economic or social potential.

Sources of Innovation

There are, of course, innovations that spring from a flash of genius. Most innovations, however, especially the successful ones, result from a conscious, purposeful search for innovation opportunities, which are found in only a few situations.

Four such areas of opportunity exist within a company or industry:

- unexpected occurrences

- incongruities

- process needs

- industry and market changes

Three additional sources of opportunity exist outside a company in its social and intellectual environment:

- demographic changes

- changes in perception

- new knowledge

True, these sources overlap, different as they may be in the nature of their risk, difficulty, and complexity, and the potential for innovation may well lie in more than one area at a time. But together, they account for the great majority of all innovation opportunities.

UNEXPECTED OCCURRENCES

Consider, first, the easiest and simplest source of innovation opportunity: the unexpected. In the early 1930s, IBM developed the first modern accounting machine, which was designed for banks. But banks in 1933 did not buy new equipment. What saved the company—according to a story that Thomas Watson, Sr., the company's founder and long-term CEO, often told—was its exploitation of an unexpected success: the New York Public Library wanted to buy a machine. Unlike the banks, libraries in those early New Deal days had money, and Watson sold more than a hundred of his otherwise unsalable machines to libraries.

Fifteen years later, when everyone believed that computers were designed for advanced scientific work, business unexpectedly showed an interest in a machine that could do payroll. Univac, which had the most advanced machine, spurned business applications. But IBM immediately realized it faced a possible unexpected success, redesigned what was basically Univac's machine for such mundane applications as payroll, and within five years became the leader in the computer industry, a position it has maintained even to this day.

The unexpected failure may be an equally important innovation-opportunity source. Everyone knows about the Ford Edsel as the biggest new-car failure in automotive history. What very few people seem to know, however, is that the Edsel's failure was the foundation for much of the company's later success. Ford planned the Edsel, the most carefully designed car to that point in American automotive history, to give the company a full product line with which to compete with General Motors. When it bombed, despite all the planning, market research, and design that had gone into it, Ford realized that something was happening in the automobile market that ran counter to the basic assumptions on which GM and everyone else had been designing and marketing cars. No longer was the market segmenting primarily by income groups; the new principle of segmentation was what we now call *lifestyles*. Ford's response was the Mustang—a car that gave the company a distinct personality and reestablished it as an industry leader.

Unexpected successes and failures are such productive sources of innovation opportunities because most businesses dismiss them, disregard them, and even resent them. The German scientist who around 1905

The attitude managers often take to the unexpected—"It should not have happened"—is further ingrained by corporate reporting systems.

synthesized novocaine, the first non-addictive narcotic, had intended it to be used in major surgical procedures like amputation. Surgeons, however, preferred total anesthesia for such procedures; they still do. Instead, novocaine found a ready appeal among dentists. Its inventor spent the remaining years of his life traveling from dental school to dental school making speeches that forbade dentists from "misusing" his noble invention in applications for which he had not intended it.

This is a caricature, to be sure, but it illustrates the attitude managers often take to the unexpected: "It should not have happened." Corporate reporting systems further ingrain this reaction, for they draw attention away from unanticipated possibilities. The typical monthly or quarterly report has on its first page a list of problems—that is, the areas where results fall short of expectations. Such information is needed, of course; it helps prevent deterioration of performance.

But it also suppresses the recognition of new opportunities. The first acknowledgment of a possible opportunity usually applies to an area in which a company does better than budgeted. Thus genuinely entrepreneurial businesses have two "first pages"—a problem page and an opportunity page—and managers spend equal time on both.

INCONGRUITIES

Alcon Laboratories was one of the success stories of the 1960s because Bill Conner, the company's cofounder, exploited an incongruity in medical technology. The cataract operation is the world's third or fourth most common surgical procedure. During the last 300 years, doctors systematized it to the point that the only "old-fashioned" step left was the cutting of a ligament. Eye surgeons had learned to cut the ligament with complete success, but it was so different a procedure from the rest of the operation, and so incompatible with it, that they often dreaded it. It was incongruous.

Doctors had known for 50 years about an enzyme that could dissolve the ligament without cutting. All Conner did was to add a preservative to this enzyme that gave it a few months' shelf life. Eye surgeons immediately accepted the new compound, and Alcon found itself with a worldwide monopoly. Fifteen years later, Nestlé bought the company for a fancy price.

Such an incongruity within the logic or rhythm of a process is only one possibility out of which innovation opportunities may arise. Another source is incongruity between economic realities. For instance, whenever an industry has a steadily growing market but falling profit margins—as, say, in the steel industries of developed countries between 1950 and 1970—an incongruity exists. The innovative response: minimills.

An incongruity between expectations and results can also open up possibilities for innovation. For 50 years after the turn of the century, shipbuilders and shipping companies worked hard both to make ships faster and to lower their fuel consumption. Even so, the more successful they were in boosting speed and trimming fuel needs, the worse the economics of ocean freighters became. By 1950 or so, the ocean freighter was dying, if not already dead.

All that was wrong, however, was an incongruity between the industry's assumptions and its realities. The real costs did not come from doing work (that is, being at sea) but from *not* doing work (that is, sitting idle in port). Once managers understood where costs truly lay, the innovations were obvious: the roll-on and roll-off ship and the container ship. These solutions, which involved old technology, simply applied to the ocean freighter what railroads and truckers had been using for 30 years. A shift in viewpoint, not in technology, totally changed the economics of ocean shipping and turned it into one of the major growth industries of the last 20 to 30 years.

PROCESS NEEDS

Anyone who has ever driven in Japan knows that the country has no modern highway system. Its roads still follow the paths laid down for—or by—oxcarts in the tenth century. What makes the system work for automobiles and trucks is an adaptation of the reflector used on American highways since the early 1930s. This reflector lets each car see which other cars are approaching from any one of a half-dozen directions. This minor invention, which enables traffic to move smoothly and with a minimum of accidents, exploited a process need.

What we now call "the media" had their origin in two innovations developed around 1890 in response to a process need. One was Ottmar Mergenthaler's Linotype, which made it possible to produce a newspaper quickly and in large volume. The other was a social innovation, modern advertising, invented by the first true newspaper publishers, Adolph Ochs of the *New York Times*, Joseph Pulitzer of the *New York World*, and William Randolph Hearst. Advertising made it possible for them to distribute news practically free of charge, with the profit coming from marketing.

INDUSTRY AND MARKET CHANGES

Managers may believe that industry structures are ordained by the Good Lord, but these structures can—and often do—change overnight. Such change creates tremendous opportunity for innovation.

One of American business's great success stories in recent decades is the brokerage firm of Donaldson, Lufkin & Jenrette, recently acquired by the Equitable

Life Assurance Society. DL&J was founded in 1960 by three young men, all graduates of the Harvard Business School, who realized that the structure of the financial industry was changing as institutional investors became dominant. These young men had practically no capital and no connections. Still, within a few years, their firm had become a leader in the move to negotiated commissions and one of Wall Street's stellar performers. It was the first to be incorporated and go public.

In a similar fashion, changes in industry structure have created massive innovation opportunities for American health-care providers. During the last 10 or 15 years, independent surgical and psychiatric clinics, emergency centers, and HMOs have opened throughout the country. Comparable opportunities in telecommunications followed industry upheavals—both in equip-

New opportunities rarely fit the way an industry has always approached the market, defined it, or organized to serve it.

ment (with the emergence of such companies as Rolm in the manufacturing of private branch exchanges) and in transmission (with the emergence of MCI and Sprint in long-distance service).

When an industry grows quickly—the critical figure seems to be in the neighborhood of 40% growth in ten years or less—its structure changes. Established companies, concentrating on defending what they already have, tend not to counterattack when a newcomer challenges them. Indeed, when market or industry structures change, traditional industry leaders again and again neglect the fastest-growing market segments. New opportunities rarely fit the way the industry has always approached the market, defined it, or organized to serve it. Innovators therefore have a good chance of being left alone for a long time.

DEMOGRAPHIC CHANGES

Of the outside sources of innovation opportunity, demographics are the most reliable. Demographic events have known lead times; for instance, every person who will be in the American labor force by the year 2000 has already been born. Yet because policy makers often neglect demographics, those who watch them and exploit them can reap great rewards.

The Japanese are ahead in robotics because they paid attention to demographics. Everyone in the developed countries around 1970 or so knew that there was both a baby bust and an education explosion going on; half or more of the young people were staying in school beyond high school. Consequently, the number of people available for traditional blue-collar work in manufacturing was bound to decrease and become inadequate by 1990. Everyone knew this, but only the Japanese acted on it, and they now have a ten-year lead in robotics.

Much the same is true of Club Mediterranee's success in the travel and resort business. By 1970, thoughtful observers could have seen the emergence of large numbers of affluent and educated young adults in Europe and the United States. Not comfortable with the kind of vacations their working-class parents had enjoyed—the summer weeks at Brighton or Atlantic City—these young people were ideal customers for a new and exotic version of the "hangout" of their teen years.

Managers have known for a long time that demographics matter, but they have always believed that population statistics change slowly. In this century, however, they don't. Indeed, the innovation opportunities made possible by changes in the numbers of people—and in their age distribution, education, occupations, and geographic location—are among the most rewarding and least risky of entrepreneurial pursuits.

CHANGES IN PERCEPTION

"The glass is half-full" and "the glass is half-empty" are descriptions of the same phenomenon but have vastly different meanings. Changing a manager's perception of a glass from half-full to half-empty opens up big innovation opportunities.

All factual evidence indicates, for instance, that in the last 20 years, Americans' health has improved with unprecedented speed—whether measured by mortality rates for the newborn, survival rates for the very old, the incidence of cancers (other than lung cancer), cancer cure rates, or other factors.

A change in perception does not alter facts. It changes their meaning, though—and quickly.

Even so, collective hypochondria grips the nation. Never before has there been so much concern with or fear about health. Suddenly, everything seems to cause cancer or degenerative heart disease or premature loss of memory. The glass is clearly half-empty.

Rather than rejoicing in great improvements in health, Americans seem to be emphasizing how far away they still are from immortality. This view of things has created many opportunities for innovations: markets for new health-care magazines, for all kinds of health foods, and for exercise classes and jogging equipment. The fastest growing new U.S. business in 1983 was a company that makes indoor exercise equipment.

A change in perception does not alter facts. It changes their meaning, though—and very quickly. It took less than two years for the computer to change from being perceived as a threat, and as something only big businesses would use, to something one buys for doing income tax. Economics do not necessarily dictate such a change; in fact, they may be irrelevant. What determines whether people see a glass as half-full or half-empty is mood rather than fact, and a change in mood often defies quantification. But it is not exotic. It is concrete. It can be defined. It can be tested. And it can be exploited for innovation opportunity.

NEW KNOWLEDGE

Among history-making innovations, those based on new knowledge—whether scientific, technical, or social—rank high. They are the superstars of entrepreneurship; they get the publicity and the money. They are what people usually mean when they talk of innovation, although not all innovations based on knowledge are important.

Knowledge-based innovations differ from all others in the time they take, in their casualty rates, and in their predictability, as well as in the challenges they pose to entrepreneurs. Like most superstars, they can be temperamental, capricious, and hard to direct. They have, for instance, the longest lead time of all innovations. There is a protracted span between the emergence of new knowledge and its distillation into usable technology. Then there is another long period before this new technology appears in the marketplace in products, processes, or services. Overall, the lead time involved is something like 50 years, a figure that has not shortened appreciably throughout history.

To become effective, innovation of this sort usually demands not one kind of knowledge but many. Consider one of the most potent knowledge-based innovations: modern banking. The theory of the entrepreneurial bank—that is, of the purposeful use of capital to generate economic development—was formulated by the Comte de Saint-Simon during the era of Napoleon. Despite Saint-Simon's extraordinary prominence, it was not until 30 years after his death in 1825 that two of his disciples, the brothers Jacob and Isaac Pereire, established the first entrepreneurial bank, the Credit Mobilier, and ushered in what we now call *finance capitalism.*

The Pereires, however, did not know modern commercial banking, which developed at about the same time across the channel in England. The Credit Mobilier failed ignominiously. A few years later, two young men—one an American, J.P. Morgan, and one a German, Georg Siemens—put together the French theory of entrepreneurial banking and the English theory of commercial banking to create the first successful modern banks, J.P. Morgan & Company in New York and the Deutsche Bank in Berlin. Ten years later, a young Japanese, Shibusawa Eiichi, adapted Siemens's concept to his country and thereby laid the foundation of Japan's modern economy. This is how knowledge-based innovation always works.

The computer, to cite another example, required no fewer than six separate strands of knowledge:

- binary arithmetic;

- Charles Babbage's conception of a calculating machine, in the first half of the nineteenth century;

- the punch card, invented by Herman Hollerith for the U.S. census of 1890;

- the audion tube, an electronic switch invented in 1906;

- symbolic logic, which was developed between 1910 and 1913 by Bertrand Russell and Alfred North Whitehead;

- concepts of programming and feedback that came out of abortive attempts during World War I to develop effective anti-aircraft guns.

Although all the necessary knowledge was available by 1918, the first operational digital computer did not appear until 1946.

Long lead times and the need for convergence among different kinds of knowledge explain the peculiar rhythm of knowledge-based innovation, its attractions, and its dangers. During a long gestation period, there is a lot of talk and little action. Then, when all the elements suddenly converge, there is tremendous excitement and activity and an enormous amount of speculation. Between 1880 and 1890, for example, almost 1,000 electric-apparatus companies were founded in developed countries. Then, as always, there was a crash and a shakeout. By 1914, only 25 were still alive. In the early 1920s, 300 to 500 automobile companies existed in the United States; by 1960, only 4 remained.

It may be difficult, but knowledge-based innovation can be managed. Success requires careful analysis of the various kinds of knowledge needed to make an innovation possible. Both J.P. Morgan and Georg Siemens did this when they established their banking ventures. The Wright brothers did this when they developed the first operational airplane.

Careful analysis of the needs—and, above all, the capabilities—of the intended user is also essential. It may seem paradoxical, but knowledge-based innovation is more market dependent than any other kind of innovation. De Havilland, a British company, designed and built the first passenger jet airplane, but it did not analyze what the market needed and therefore did not identify two key factors. One was configuration—that is, the right size with the right payload for the routes on which a jet would give an airline the greatest advantage. The other was equally mundane: how could the airlines finance the purchase of such an expensive plane? Because de Havilland failed to do an adequate user analysis, two American companies, Boeing and Douglas, took over the commercial jet-aircraft industry.

The greatest praise an innovation can receive is for people to say: "This is obvious!"

Principles of Innovation

Purposeful, systematic innovation begins with the analysis of the sources of new opportunities. Depending on the context, sources will have different importance at different times. Demographics, for instance, may be of little concern to innovators of fundamental industrial processes like steelmaking, although Mergenthaler's Linotype machine became successful primarily because there were not enough skilled typesetters available to satisfy a mass market. By the same token, new knowledge may be of little relevance to someone innovating a social instrument to satisfy a need that changing demographics or tax laws have created. But—whatever the situation—innovators must analyze all opportunity sources.

Because innovation is both conceptual and perceptual, would-be innovators must also go out and look, ask, and listen. Successful innovators use both the right and left sides of their brains. They look at figures. They look at people. They work out analytically what the innovation has to be to satisfy an opportunity. Then they go out and look at potential users to study their expectations, their values, and their needs.

To be effective, an innovation has to be simple, and it has to be focused. It should do only one thing; otherwise it confuses people. Indeed, the greatest praise an innovation can receive is for people to say, "This is obvious! Why didn't I think of it? It's so simple!" Even the innovation that creates new users and new markets should be directed toward a specific, clear, and carefully designed application.

Effective innovations start small. They are not grandiose. They try to do one specific thing. It may be to enable a moving vehicle to draw electric power while it runs along rails, the innovation that made possible the electric streetcar. Or it may be the elementary idea of putting the same number

If an innovation does not aim at leadership from the beginning, it is unlikely to be innovative enough.

of matches into a matchbox (it used to be 50). This simple notion made possible the automatic filling of matchboxes and gave the Swedes a world monopoly on matches for half a century. By contrast, grandiose ideas for things that will "revolutionize an industry" are unlikely to work.

In fact, no one can foretell whether a given innovation will end up a big business or a modest achievement. But even if the results are modest, the successful innovation aims from the beginning to become the standard setter, to determine the direction of a new technology or a new industry, to create the business that is—and remains—ahead of the pack. If an innovation does not aim at leadership from the beginning, it is unlikely to be innovative enough.

Above all, innovation is work rather than genius. It requires knowledge. It often requires ingenuity. And it requires focus. There are clearly people who are more talented as innovators than others, but their talents lie in well-defined areas. Indeed, innovators rarely work in more than one area. For all his systematic innovative accomplishments, Thomas Edison worked only in the electrical field. An innovator in financial areas, Citibank for example, is not likely to embark on innovations in health care.

In innovation, as in any other endeavor, there is talent, there is ingenuity, and there is knowledge. But when all is said and done, what innovation requires is hard, focused, purposeful work. If diligence, persistence, and commitment are lacking, talent, ingenuity, and knowledge are of no avail.

There is, of course, far more to entrepreneurship than systematic innovation—distinct entrepreneurial strategies, for example, and the principles of entrepreneurial management, which are needed equally in the established enterprise, the public service organization, and the new venture. But the very foundation of entrepreneurship—as a practice and as a discipline—is the practice of systematic innovation.

Originally published in May–June 1985; revised in November–December 1998
Reprint 98604

Interpretive Management

What General Managers Can Learn from Design

RICHARD K. LESTER, MICHAEL J. PIORE,
AND KAMAL M. MALEK

Executive Summary

THE PAST TWO DECADES have seen a dramatic acceleration in the pace of marketplace change. Companies have abandoned the old hierarchical model, with its clean functional divisions and clear lines of authority, and adopted flatter, less bureaucratic structures. But if most organizations have begun to adapt to the uncertainty of rapid change, most managers have not. They remain locked into the mechanical mind-set of the industrial age—that is, they assume that any management challenge can be translated to a clearly defined problem for which an optimal solution can be found.

That approach works in stable markets and even in markets that change in predictable ways. Today's markets, however, are increasingly unstable and unpredictable. Managers can never know precisely what they're trying to achieve or how best to achieve it. They can't even define the problem, much less engineer a solution.

The challenges facing the general manger in these circumstances, the authors argue, resemble those typically confronted by design managers. In the unpredictable world of research and design, neither the flow of the development process nor its end point can be defined at the outset. Rather than the traditional *analytical* approach to management, the design world requires an *interpretive* one. And that approach is equally well suited to rapidly changing, unpredictable markets. The authors describe how companies such as Levi Strauss & Company and Chiron Corporation have stayed at the top of their industries by adopting just such an interpretive approach to management.

As the pace of marketplace change has accelerated over the past two decades, we have seen a dramatic shift in the nature of business organizations. Companies have abandoned the old hierarchical model, with its clean functional divisions and clear lines of authority, and adopted flatter, less bureaucratic structures. The watchword of these new organizations is *flexibility*. The goal is to adapt quickly to changes while ensuring that all the pieces of the organization are able to work together effectively, without the need for a long chain of command.

But if most organizations have begun to adapt to uncertainty, most managers have not. They remain locked into the mechanical, engineering mind-set of the industrial age. They set fixed, quantified goals—a 5%

reduction in manufacturing costs, a 99.5% accuracy rate in order fulfillment, a 15 point gain in customer satisfaction—and they "engineer" the organizational structures and processes required

Today's fast-paced markets evolve in unforeseeable ways with unforeseeable consequences.

to achieve those goals in the most efficient manner possible. They assume, in other words, that any management challenge can be translated into a clearly defined problem for which an optimal solution can be designed.

This management approach works well in markets that are stable and even in those that change in predictable ways. Today's markets, however, are increasingly unstable and unpredictable. They evolve in unforeseeable ways with unforeseeable consequences. Confronted with this kind of radical uncertainty, managers can never know precisely what they're trying to achieve or how best to achieve it. They can't even define the problem, much less engineer a solution. A company may successfully hit its targets for reducing manufacturing costs, improving order-fulfillment accuracy, or boosting customer satisfaction only to discover that a new technology or a new competitor has rendered its entire business obsolete.

The challenge facing the general manager under these circumstances begins to resemble the challenge that the manager of new-product development has always confronted. In the unpredictable world of research and design, neither the flow of the development process nor its end point can be defined at the outset. The shape of the new product changes, often dramatically, as the effort to create it proceeds. A strictly mechanical approach to management, with its stress on clearly defined objectives, roles, and structures, would kill the creativity that lies at the heart of design. Success in new-product development requires a different kind of management and a different kind of manager.

Two Approaches to Management

Does the experience of design managers hold practical lessons for general managers who are facing increasing uncertainty in their own businesses? With that question in mind, we studied the product development activities of companies in a number of rapidly changing industries, such as cellular telephones, medical devices, automobiles, and apparel. We found two sharply contrasting approaches to management, which we term *analytical* and *interpretive*. While the analytical approach reflects the traditional managerial perspective, the interpretive approach involves a new perspective, one highly suited to rapidly changing, unpredictable markets. Both approaches are valid, but each serves very different purposes and calls for very different organizational strategies and managerial skills.

Under the analytical approach, the design of a new product is viewed as essentially an engineering challenge—as a problem that must be solved. The analytical manager seeks to define a clear objective, usually based on research into customer needs, and he identifies the resources—human, financial, and technical—available to meet that goal, as well as the constraints on those resources. The manager then divides the problem into a series of discrete components and assigns each one to a knowledgeable specialist. A dishwasher manufacturer, for example, may have market research indicating that customers are placing an increasingly high premium on low water consumption and quiet operation. In response, the company will set strict goals for reducing water usage and noise in its next generation of products. The product development leader will then assign different elements of the design problem to experts in materials, chemistry, industrial design, acoustics, and other relevant disciplines. The solution is ultimately obtained by integrating all the components in some optimal combination. The entire development effort is viewed as a single project, which must be brought to closure as quickly and efficiently as possible.

But not all the activity that takes place in product development can be accommodated within such a tightly structured analytical framework. Frequently, for example, the customer doesn't really know what he wants or needs—as is the case today in everything from electronic commerce to biotechnology to home entertainment. Indeed, it is often more accurate to think of the customer as having no preexisting needs at all. Those needs instead emerge out of a series of interactions, or conversations, during which the customer and the designer together discover something about the customer's life and how the new product might fit into it. The features of the product emerge in the same way—through an ongoing give-and-take between the customer and the company, and among the various members of the product development team, including manufacturing and marketing. Nothing is fixed at the outset: not the customer's needs, not the product itself, not even the product's components or the elements of the manufacturing system.

The manager of an interpretive organization needs to act like the leader of a jazz combo.

When there is such a high degree of uncertainty, the development effort is better understood as an open-ended *process* rather than as a project in which a specific problem is solved. The role of the design organization is not so much one of analysis or problem solving as it is of *interpreting* the new situation—listening to and talking with customers and technical experts and discerning the new possibilities that open up through those interactions. Interpretation, no less than invention, is a highly creative process. To encourage and harness that creativity, the manager of the interpretive organization needs to act less like an engineer and more like the leader of a jazz combo. Diverse components need to be brought together—musicians, instruments, solos, themes, tempos, an audience—but their roles and their relationships are changing all the time. The goal is not to arrive at a fixed and final shape but to channel the work in a way that both influences and fulfills the listener's—the customer's—expectations. The interpretive manager, unlike the analytical manager, embraces ambiguity and improvisation as essential to innovation. She seeks openings, not endings. (See "The View through the Interpretive Lens" at the end of this article.)

Many of the best examples of interpretive management in product development can be found in the fashion apparel industry, where customers' tastes are always in flux. Although fashion design does involve well-defined projects—garments must, after all, be created within strict seasonal deadlines—these projects do not form the essence of the development effort. The core of fashion is the process by which the idea of what is fashionable develops. Fashion is not a "problem" that is "solved" in the course of a discrete project. Rather, the sense of what is fashionable emerges from a series of conversations among fashion designers, clothing buyers, key customers, garment manufacturers, and fashion writers. The conversations have neither a beginning nor an end. The question of what is fashionable has no final answer. On the contrary, the whole idea is that the answer keeps changing. New creations—that is, new garments—emerge continually, drawn out of an unfolding, open-ended process. Without this process, there could be no individual projects.

Levi's Conversations

One of the fastest-growing fashion companies of recent years is Levi Strauss & Company. Ironically, for the first century of its existence, Levi's never thought of itself as a fashion company at all. Its product—one-style-suits-all denim work pants—was a commodity. In fact, Levi's jeans can be considered a prototypical commodity of mass consumption in the United States, the Model T of the garment industry. Although clothing production has always been difficult to mechanize, the cutting and sewing of jeans was as close to assembly line production as could be found in the outer garment industry.

But the jeans business changed dramatically in the late 1970s, when fashion suddenly started to play a central role. Pricey designer jeans in a multitude of styles proliferated. Denim clothing became a staple not just of work life but of night life. Seeing an opportunity to sell its products at much higher margins, Levi's moved to take advantage of this trend, with great success. In the ensuing years, the company evolved into a true fashion leader, branching out from its traditional jeans line to its highly successful Dockers line of casual clothes and to its new Slates line of dress pants. Adept at anticipating and managing the evolution of style, Levi's posted ten consecutive years of record sales between 1986 and 1996, as its revenues grew from $2.7 billion to $7.1 billion. In recent months, in response to weakening demand for apparel, Levi's has moved aggressively to further sharpen its focus on the fashion end of its business.

In transforming itself from a commodity manufacturer to a fashion company, Levi's has invested heavily in product development. Several times a year, the company prepares new collections for its major product lines. It thinks of these collections in terms of a V-shaped merchandising model. At the back of the store are the standard, perennial items—the backbone of the collection, which generates the bulk of the revenue. These items change little from year to year. At the very front of the store are new items just introduced into the collection, aimed at the fashion-conscious consumer and often geared to a particular season. In the middle are a set of items introduced in earlier collections that have sold well but have not yet earned a place in the company's permanent collection. Products move from the front of the store to the back over their life cycle, and they may be dropped from the collection at any time.

In many ways, Levi's method of preparing its collections is consistent with the analytical mode of product development. The effort is organized in a series of distinct phases. There are definite start and end dates, and there are "gates" through which the collection must pass as it moves toward the market. Once a design has been introduced and has spent some time on store shelves, its fate can be predicted fairly accurately, and decisions about it can be structured analytically based on hard data.

For the fashion items at the front of the store, however, the analytical approach won't work. There is simply too much uncertainty about fashion trends, customer reactions, and even manufacturing capabilities. Levi's manages the generation of these new-product ideas very differently from the way it manages the collection as a whole. It stresses interpreting customer needs and production capabilities, not simply analyzing them.

For its jeans line, Levi's looks in two different directions for product innovations. One is toward the consumer. The other is toward the finishing process, which in large part determines the look and feel of the garment. In working with both the consumer and the finishing process, the design leader plays a critical managerial role for which there is no term in the analytical lexicon. One way to think about that role is as guiding the flow of a conversation.

For Levi's, the notion of a conversation with the consumer is more than just a metaphor. The company divides the market into age segments and assigns a designer to each segment. The designer is encouraged to become immersed in the segment's culture, to live the life of its members. She goes shopping at the stores where they shop, eats in their restaurants, dances in their clubs, listens to their radio stations, reads their magazines—all in an effort to pick out new trends. The conversation is extended into the company itself through meetings at which the designers discuss what they have seen and what they think it means, comparing developments in the lifestyles of different generations.

Levi's strives to be an active participant in conversations with consumers of jeans.

Levi's is an effective listener, but it is by no means just a listener. Rather, it strives to be an active participant in the conversation. Take the case of baggy jeans— a fashion trend that emerged from the youth culture of the inner city, where it became a hallmark of rap singers and their fans. Levi's concluded early on that the trend would spread to the general culture as rap music itself grew in popularity, and the company invested heavily in designs rooted in the trend. But the market began to level off much earlier than the company had expected. At that point, Levi's launched an intensive advertising campaign around the rap theme. The campaign succeeded in generating a second, larger wave of demand for the new fashion, particularly among suburban teenagers. Did Levi's create the baggy jeans fashion? Not exactly. Company managers were not sure why the advertising campaign worked, and they by no means viewed its success as preordained. What is certain, though, is that Levi's advertising was itself as much a part of youth culture as the rap music with which the baggy jeans were originally associated. To the analytical manager, Levi's success would seem to be the product of a mysterious chemistry, an unmanageable chain of serendipitous events. But the fact is that Levi's, by pursuing an open-ended, unstructured form of interpretive management, instigated and guided that chain of events to create a winning product.

The other source of innovation for Levi's jeans is the finishing process. Because current jeans fashions are heavily influenced by a manufacturer's ability to replicate the look and feel of used garments, finishing is central to product development. The basic technology of finishing is straightforward: a garment is laundered to soften its fabric and texture, to alter its fit, and to change its color—all in ways that aren't easily produced by chemicals and dyes. In addition, finished garments are typically abraded by washing them with stones or pumice or by brushing or sandblasting them in order to produce the lines and creases of used clothes. As much as 80% of the life of a garment is expended in the finishing process.

Because finishing is an inexact science, getting jeans with the desired features into retail stores in a timely manner requires close and continual collaboration among the designers and manufacturers of the garment, the textile mills that supply the denim, the laundries that perform the finishing, and the machine shops that produce the equipment used by the laundries. Experimentation with new techniques is constant, both to create new effects and to reproduce effects already achieved in other ways. The introduction of new techniques has led to a cascade of changes in cooperating industries. Denim fabric has been redesigned to withstand extensive abrasion. Industrial washing machines have been redesigned to stand up to the pounding delivered by the stones and pumice, and they have been equipped with computer controls to adjust to different kinds of stones. The combination of changes in fabrics, techniques, and equipment can itself produce new and unexpected effects, leading to further discovery, further experimentation, and further change.

Where so much turns on happenstance, a strictly analytical approach to management would be counterproductive. The analyst's stress on closure would tend to freeze the process, cutting off the continuing stream of discoveries that leads to new leaps in fashion. Not surprisingly, Levi's has come to take as conversational an approach to working with finishers as it takes to learning about customers. A particularly key role in this process has been played by one of the company's outside laundries, American Garment Finishers of El Paso, Texas, and its president, Claude Blankiet. Blankiet combines a formal technical education—he was trained as a chemical engineer—with a strong intuitive sense for fashion and design. He is widely credited with exceptional judgment about the marketability of new effects achieved in the finishing process. Moreover, he is a living example of the interpretive manager.

Over the years, Blankiet has developed an extensive network of contacts in the jeans industry across Asia, Europe, and the United States that helps him stay on top of technical developments. He travels extensively, visiting other laundries as well as washing-machine manufacturers and fabric and garment makers in order to exchange tricks of the trade. By gathering the experiences of others, he expands his own repertoire of techniques for producing or reproducing desired effects; he also pushes the entire finishing industry forward.

Levi's has begun to rely on Blankiet to strengthen communication among its own laundries and laboratories, which has been hampered by a tradition of rivalry and competition. Although these facilities have regularly encountered similar technical problems, they have shared little information. To ensure that popular garments can be produced reliably in large quantities, Levi's wants to improve the ability of laundries to reproduce effects created at other laundries. From the analytical perspective, Blankiet's task is to work out a technical solution to the problem of achieving each desired new finish and then standardize the knowledge and procedures across the network of laundries. But Blankiet's own understanding of his role is more consistent with the interpretive view. Because finishing technology is still highly empirical, without a firm theoretical base, new effects are often achieved inadvertently. Blankiet sees himself as an interpreter who instigates and translates wide-ranging conversations among the laundries. While he helps Levi's achieve better communication among its laundries, he personally seeks not to eliminate the variations in finishing but to exploit those variations as a continuing source of new ideas and insights.

Recently, Levi's jeans appear to have lost a step on the street fashion scene. The company has been slow to exploit the wide-leg jeans style, the latest big fashion trend, and younger consumers have been leaving the brand for other fashion-focused merchandisers. Why did Levi's miss the emerging trend? One reason may be that its fast-growing fashion-jeans division has become more structured and formal and has lost some of its earlier flexibility and receptivity to new fashion ideas. The company is now moving to recreate what has been lost. It is setting up another smaller fashion unit and is taking steps to renew the flow of fashion ideas that links the company to the street, to its finishers, and to the rest of the world. In effect, Levi's is seeking to reintroduce the interpretive dimension of management that is so critical to the success of fashion-driven businesses.

Beyond Fashion

Fashion apparel is hardly a typical industry, of course, but many of its characteristics are now being replicated in other, very different industries. In many consumer-product and service sectors, for example, managers are struggling with unpredictable shifts in customer needs and unforeseen changes in technology that require a steady stream of new and different products. Even Andy Grove, CEO of the archetypal analytical company, Intel, whose product-development activities are dominated by huge design projects with thousands of people racing against tight deadlines to get the latest generation of chips to market, has acknowledged "a deep-seated conviction that our business has some of the characteristics of the fashion industry. You always have to come up with something exciting and new to stay on top." No matter what industry a company competes in, the greater its susceptibility to shifting tastes and technologies, the greater the risk of relying wholly on an analytical style of management.

The need for an interpretive approach tends to be particularly strong in markets or industries that are still in their formative stages. A good recent example is the cellular telephone industry. At the outset, the market for cellular phones was undefined. Even the role the technology would play could not be predicted. Was a cellular phone a toy, or was it a genuine alternative to traditional wire-line systems? Was it basically a car radio, or was it a portable, handheld device? Would demand for the service be limited to a few narrow segments, or would it be universal? The nature of a cellular system, the different components of the infrastructure, the technologies used, the functions provided, the character of competition, the economics of the business—all were unclear.

The companies that have come to dominate the cellular industry all initially managed their cellular divisions using a highly interpretive approach. AT&T housed its cellular operations in Bell Labs, encouraging a climate of open-ended experimentation and discovery. Motorola organized its initial efforts around a core of engineers who operated as a flexible, ad hoc team, drawing in other members of the organization as needed and conversing directly with customers about their needs and desired product features. Matsushita's cellular unit lacked clear functional boundaries, thus encouraging communication between its product-development and manufacturing units. Nokia's cellular business began as a highly entrepreneurial operation with informal design procedures. Salespeople communicated directly with the product development team, often making last-minute changes to product specifications in response to customers' requests.

Once the market began to stabilize in the middle and late 1980s, each of these companies began to reorganize its cellular division, imposing much more formal structures with much more analytical managerial approaches. The transition was most dramatic at AT&T and Matsushita. AT&T moved its cellular operations out of Bell Labs, establishing a stand-alone business unit, Network Wireless Systems, led by experienced managers drawn from other operating divisions. It also introduced a formal five-step product-development process based on a model used throughout the company. Matsushita brought in a manager from its television division to oversee the cellular business and established a clearly defined hand-off point between development and manufacturing, instituting an analytical review to ensure that the product was ready to go into mass production. Motorola and Nokia also embraced a more analytical approach, but they did not abandon the interpretive perspective entirely. Motorola limited customers' access to the development team by appointing a set of project managers to act as points of contact, but these project managers continued to play an interpretive role in communicating between developers and customers. Nokia instituted a formal product-development process with well-defined phases marked by analytical reviews, but it still encouraged cross-functional conversations throughout the process.

When these companies began their shift from the interpretive to the analytical approach, they shared a belief that the cellular business was stabilizing, with increasingly well-defined customer needs and product features. In hindsight, we can see that their assumption was wrong. The cellular business has entered a new period of radical uncertainty. A number of technological, regulatory, and competitive developments— the introduction of personal communications service,

Adopting a purely analytical approach as a market matures is common but not always correct.

the growing communications power of personal digital assistants and pagers, the expanding range of cordless phones, the development of satellite systems—have converged in a way that couldn't be predicted, again casting into doubt the ultimate role that traditional cellular service will play. It may turn out that the four leading competitors, particularly AT&T and Matsushita, acted too quickly in shifting away from their original interpretive approach to management.

The instinct displayed by the cellular competitors—to move to an analytical approach as a market matures—is a common one. After all, as a business grows larger and more complex, its efficiency depends on the establishment of well-defined operating processes and formal management structures. Strong analytical, problem-solving skills become more and more important to effective management. Nevertheless, as radical uncertainty becomes a more pervasive feature of the business environment—as it has in the cellular business—the limitations of a *strictly* analytical model will become progressively more debilitating. The most successful managers will understand both approaches, seeing them as complementary, not antagonistic, and they will be capable of striking a sensible balance between the two.

A Different Way of Seeing

Few managers today are capable of taking such a balanced view. Because the pull of the analytical approach is so powerful and its routines so ingrained into management practice, most managers simply can't comprehend the possibility of a different approach. Even at fashion-oriented Levi's, one senior manager told us he looked forward to the day when interpretive conversations among the company's denim finishers would no longer be necessary. He hoped to introduce more scientific knowledge into the finishing process, cross-training designers in relevant technical disciplines so that they would be able to develop and standardize new finishes quickly. He wanted his designers to work "scientifically—the way they do it in biotechnology."

Interestingly, though, product development in the biotech industry is not always "scientific" in the way the Levi's manager used the term. Indeed, it sometimes closely resembles the Levi's model of product development. Chiron Corporation, a leading biotech company headquartered directly across the San Francisco Bay from Levi's, provides a good example. Although Chiron uses analytical structures in many areas of its business, its chief executive has embraced an explicitly interpretive role, positioning himself and his company at the center of an extensive network of university and corporate researchers. His strategy has been to draw scientists from all parts of the biotechnology community into a continuing exchange of information with his company's people. To carve out its position as the central node in the research community, Chiron has often had to share its own information about evolving technologies and commercial applications, with the expectation that its interlocutors would divulge information of their own. Outside researchers now routinely seek out the company's researchers to discuss new findings and get advice on new technical problems—a pattern of communication that the company views as one of its major strategic assets.

Chiron's approach mirrors the way Claude Blankiet draws new members into his network of laundries. When Blankiet spots technical problems during his visits to outside laundries, he offers unsolicited solutions in the hope that the laundry will reciprocate by sharing technical secrets of its own. His exchanges, like those of Chiron's researchers, could be viewed from the analytical perspective as transactions wherein information of more or less equal value is traded. But from the interpretive view, they can be understood as the opening gambit in an ongoing conversation.

The idea that the same activity can be at once analytical and interpretive might seem illogical at first. But just as modern physics instructs us to think about light as both particles and waves, so too can a business organization be looked at from either the analytical or the interpretive perspective. One view may be more immediately useful in certain circumstances—as uncertainty increases, for example, the emphasis on interpretation should grow—but the simultaneous use of both lenses will provide managers with deeper insights into their challenges, opening up new possibilities for action.

Consider, for example, the concept of core competency. When a company sets out to determine what it does best, it typically takes an iterative approach, cycling between what it *can* do given its existing resources and what it *might* do given the opportunities presented in the marketplace. This back-and-forth process, essentially interpretive in nature, is almost always fruitful, revealing new possibilities as well as new constraints. Too often, though, companies rush to end the process: "These are our core capabilities, and these are the products we will produce, and these are the processes we will use to produce them." The analyst's need for closure terminates the interpreter's search for knowledge. The risk is that, in an unpredictable environment, this kind of closure can be disastrous. The company can end up doing a very good job producing products no one wants to buy.

Interpretive managers, by contrast, constantly question the boundaries of their company's core competency and sometimes even deliberately stray across those boundaries. For example, several manufacturing companies we studied—Matsushita in cellular telephones, Levi's in fashion apparel, Oticon in medical devices— maintain small retail divisions. These divisions are probably not profitable, and they certainly lie outside their companies' areas of core competency. But they provide direct exposure to the consumer, enabling the companies to test new-product ideas and to gather the kind of unfiltered information that cannot be supplied by independent retailers. The existence of these outlets cannot be justified through the analytical approach the companies use to evaluate their regular wholesale and retail channels. They can be understood only in an interpretive framework.

Toward a New Vocabulary

Interpretive management implies a whole new way of thinking about the work of business executives.

Interpretive managers, like Chiron's chief executive, identify and bring together individuals within and outside the company who might have something interesting to say to one another. They arrange, in other words, who should talk to whom. They also take an active role in influencing what people talk about—highlighting, for example, areas or experiences people have in common. Acting much like the host of a party, they introduce new people into groups where conversation seems to be flagging, intervene to suggest a new topic when the people don't seem to be able to discover what they have in common, break up groups that are headed for an unpleasant argument, and guide the conversations in a general direction without seeming (or wanting) to dictate the outcome. (See "The Work of Interpretation" at the end of this article.)

As anyone who has hosted a party knows, these are difficult skills to master. Indeed, for most managers, the interpretive approach remains an entirely foreign concept. It is not taught as an explicit discipline in business schools, it is not part of most executive training programs, and there are few role models available. Until now, we haven't even had a vocabulary for talking about the interpretive approach. As a result, managers often come to important tasks with blinders on, not recognizing even the possibility of an alternative to the analytical approach. Challenges that might more usefully have been treated as open-ended processes, where multiple possibilities could coexist and play off one another, are forced back into the analytical mold—where the emphasis is on clarification, on getting things straight, on eliminating the

By purging our organizations of what is ambiguous, we risk losing our sense of what is possible.

redundant, the ambiguous, and the unknown. The danger is that the rush to clarify often leads to the reification of insight, to the premature freezing of ideas—to the elimination, in fact, of the very conditions that are needed for creativity to flourish. By purging our organizations of what is ambiguous, we risk losing our sense of what is possible.

This is not a risk that concerns most managers today. In fact, managers fear the paralysis of indecision, the danger of *not* deciding on a course of action, more than the elimination of options. They are acutely aware that organizations need closure, otherwise nothing will be accomplished. They try to structure projects that can yield optimal solutions in the face of potentially overwhelming uncertainty. And they have a very well-developed analytical apparatus for doing this. But what they lack—and what the interpretive approach offers—is a way to keep things moving forward *without* closure, a framework that sees in ambiguity the seeds not of paralysis but of opportunity.

The View through the Interpretive Lens

FROM THE PERSPECTIVE OF the interpretive manager, many traditional business practices and institutions take on a very different look. Consider, for example, how the interpretive lens might change our view of management education, corporate research and development, and the research university.

Management Education

Management education is frequently criticized for failing to imbue students with the creativity required for effective leadership and strategic thinking. Some critics go so far as to claim that the current stress on analytical problem solving "breeds out" the creative dimensions of management—the dimensions that successful leaders tend to describe not in analytical terms but in terms of vision, inspiration, and instinct. The common response to this critique is that creativity cannot be taught. Creative managers are born, not made.

The interpretive perspective challenges that view. It shifts attention away from individualistic notions of creativity, from "isolated genius" theories of innovation, and toward an understanding of creativity as a social process. It suggests a way of thinking about the creativity of organizations—of communities—rather than the creativity of individuals, and it places a new stress on orchestration and interpretation as leadership styles. The implication for education is clear: to train interpretive leaders, management teaching would need to be broadened, focusing on developing not only problem-solving skills but also the humanistic skills traditionally associated with the more interpretive fields of literature, history, and anthropology. Management would need to be viewed as much as a liberal art as a science.

Corporate Research and Development

The ongoing debate over the role of corporate R&D, and especially that of central research laboratories, is marked by two contradictory trends. Most U.S. companies that own central labs have been shrinking or dismantling them, redirecting much of their remaining R&D activity toward the shorter-term product-development needs of their business units. Meanwhile, many Japanese companies are moving in the opposite direction, seeking to build up their central labs. They have come to view their traditional reliance on other countries to make fundamental discoveries as a disadvantageous, unsustainable strategy. It is easy to view these events as reflecting competing views of the relative merits of centralization and decentralization in the organization of in-house research. The interpretive approach, though, would lead us to focus less on the organizational structure per se and more on the role of the in-house R&D unit in orchestrating conversations between the company's business units on the one hand and the outside research community on the other.

From the interpretive perspective, the oft-told tale of Xerox's Palo Alto Research Center (PARC) takes on a different aspect. Xerox's inability to capitalize on PARC's technological breakthroughs, including its pioneering research into the graphical user interface, is often used as a lesson in the failure of central research laboratories. The blame is typically placed on PARC's close ties to Silicon Valley, which surrounded the lab and ultimately came to commercialize many of its innovations. PARC, according to this view, gave away the store. But from the interpretive perspective, PARC's relationships with outside researchers may have been not a weakness but a strength—the relationships actually underpinned the lab's breakthroughs. The failure might lie instead in the parent company's inability to integrate the lab with its business units. The interpretive manager would have sought ways to link corporate R&D more closely to the product divisions *without* weakening its relationships with the larger technical community. The lesson for the Japanese companies now investing in central laboratories, the interpretive manager would argue, is that if these labs are isolated from the broader research community, they will be much less likely to succeed.

The Research University

The interpretive view also places academic research in a different light. As the federal government slashes its research funding, U.S. research universities are wrestling with their future role. They are, in particular, looking to industry to make up for the loss in government dollars. They are finding, however, that many companies will provide funding only under proprietary research agreements.

As universities negotiate their future with government and industry sponsors, they should never lose sight of the role they are best suited to play in research and development. Once again, the interpretive approach can be illuminating. It suggests that the current positions of both the government and the commercial sector, if taken to their logical conclusion, would likely be self-defeating. On the one hand, the interpretive perspective counsels against imposing a sharp separation between basic and applied research, arguing instead that the health of the overall R&D system depends on close, intense interactions between the two disciplines. On the other hand, the interpretive viewpoint makes clear that the most important contribution the research university can make to industry, above and beyond the quantity and quality of its graduates, is to help expose private companies to a broad range of new ideas. A company that demands an exclusive, proprietary research relationship may not only be damaging the university, it may also be reducing the value that it will ultimately derive from that relationship.

The Work of Interpretation

THE WORK OF THE INTERPRETIVE MANAGER is very different from that of the analytical manager. Success requires not only a new outlook but also a new set of skills. We would make the following suggestions to managers looking to incorporate an interpretive approach into their day-to-day jobs.

Look for new ways to promote conversations about the future

Because conversation is so central to interpretation, you need to create forums and stimuli for productive, far-ranging conversations. IBM's research division, for example, recently directed its basic scientists to get out of the laboratory and start spending time with customers. "We don't want Capuchin monks in a monastery on a hill," explained former IBM research chief Jim McGroddy. "Rather, we want Franciscans in the street." The visits enable the scientists to solve customers' problems, but that's not their only benefit. The scientists themselves are changed by the experience; they gain a new perspective on their work that can lead to research breakthroughs back in the lab. Recalled McGroddy, "Recently, I ran into a couple of our mathematicians in the parking lot who were on their way to see a customer. Neither of them had visited a customer before, but we set it up for them and made it easy. They came back very excited by what they'd seen, and that affects the research agenda of our division." In a similar vein, Andersen Consulting has created several virtual business environments around the world—simulations of futuristic supermarkets, retail outlets, even entire companies—where consultants can meet and talk with their clients about what new technology might help them achieve in the future. The point of these sites is not to predict what will happen but rather to stimulate thinking and discussion about what might happen.

Many people, especially engineers, are uncomfortable with the notion of open-ended, creative conversations.

Therefore, you will often need to find ways to kick-start conversations. One conversational gambit that can be highly successful is the adoption of a so-called stretch goal. Whether that goal is actually achieved or not is often immaterial; the point is to force the enterprise out of its customary ways of working, to keep it moving and searching. One of the most famous stretch goals was the 6-Sigma quality target established by Motorola during the 1980s. As long-time Motorola chairman Bob Galvin explained in a recent interview, "It doesn't really matter what the goal is exactly, as long as it is reasonable. The point is to stimulate, to catalyze." Motorola did not, in fact, reach its target, but the 6-Sigma program stimulated many new and highly beneficial collaborations within the company (and later also with its suppliers), a large fraction of which were unanticipated at the outset.

Pick your interlocutors carefully

It's not enough just to talk; you need to talk with the right people. A number of equipment supply companies, for example, spend a lot of time with their lead clients—those customers that have leadership positions in their industry or that use the equipment in the most demanding or most innovative ways. A good lead client is a good interlocutor, capable of moving the conversation forward and widening the circle by bringing in others from its market segment. In the medical devices industry, companies developing new products seek to place the technology first with key users—practitioners with strong reputations in the professional community who will use the innovation in clinical trials and write papers disseminating the results.

A similar principle applies to the selection of suppliers. Instead of rebidding its parts purchases every year or so to find the lowest-cost producers, Chrysler now carefully selects one or two key suppliers for each component early on. The goal is not necessarily to select the lowest-cost supplier but rather to find partners who are able and willing to help advance the design of the component throughout the full production life of the vehicle.

Develop *alloy people* within your organization

In companies facing rapidly changing markets, the role of interpreters—people who can facilitate communication across organizational boundaries—is especially important. In the analytical view, communication is thought of as the exchange of packets of unambiguous information—like Morse code. It requires no interpretation to be understood. More commonly, though, the cultural and linguistic gap between different organizational units is wide, and the message must be interpreted. People who are able to bridge the gaps need to be identified and then encouraged, formally or informally, to act as interpreters. In one company we've studied, the managers and engineers who perform this key function are nicknamed *alloy people*. Just as an alloy is an amalgam of two or more metals, an alloy person represents the union of two or more points of view.

Originally published in March–April 1998
Reprint 98207

Value Innovation

The Strategic Logic of High Growth

W. CHAN KIM AND RENÉE MAUBORGNE

Executive Summary

WHY ARE SOME COMPANIES able to sustain high growth in revenues and profits—and others are not? To answer that question, the authors, both of INSEAD, spent five years studying more than 30 companies around the world. They found that the difference between the high-growth companies and their less successful competitors was in each group's assumptions about strategy. Managers of the less successful companies followed conventional strategic logic. Managers of the high-growth companies followed what the authors call the logic of *value innovation*.

Conventional strategic logic and value innovation differ along the basic dimensions of strategy. Many companies take their industry's conditions as given; value innovators don't. Many companies let competitors set the parameters of their strategic thinking; value innovators do not use rivals as benchmarks. Rather than focus on the differences among customers, value innovators look for what customers value in common. Rather than view opportunities through the lens of existing assets and capabilities, value innovators ask, What if we start anew?

The authors tell the story of the French hotelier Accor, which discarded the notion of what a hotel is supposed to look like in order to offer what most customers want: a good night's sleep at a low price. And Virgin Atlantic challenged industry conventions by eliminating first-class service and channeling savings into innovations for business-class passengers. Those companies didn't set out to build advantages over the competition, but they ended up achieving the greatest competitive advantages.

AFTER A DECADE of downsizing and increasingly intense competition, profitable growth is a tremendous challenge many companies face. Why do some companies achieve sustained high growth in both revenues and profits? In a five-year study of high-growth companies and their less successful competitors, we found that the answer lies in the way each group approached strategy. The difference in approach was not a matter of managers choosing one analytical tool or planning model over another. The difference was in the companies' fundamental, implicit assumptions about strategy. The less successful companies took a conventional approach: their strategic thinking was dominated by the idea of staying ahead of the competition. In stark contrast, the high-growth companies paid little attention to matching or beating their rivals. Instead, they sought to make their competitors irrelevant through a strategic logic we call *value innovation*. (See "Researching the Roots of High Growth" at the end of this article.)

Consider Bert Claeys, a Belgian company that operates movie theaters. From the 1960s to the 1980s, the movie theater industry in Belgium was declining steadily. With the spread of videocassette recorders and satellite and cable television, the average Belgian's moviegoing dropped from eight to two times per year. By the 1980s, many cinema operators (COs) were forced to shut down.

The COs that remained found themselves competing head-to-head for a shrinking market. All took similar actions. They turned cinemas into multiplexes with as many as ten screens, broadened their film offerings to attract all customer segments, expanded their food and drink services, and increased showing times.

Those attempts to leverage existing assets became irrelevant in 1988, when Bert Claeys created Kinepolis. Neither an ordinary cinema nor a multiplex, Kinepolis is the world's first megaplex, with 25 screens and 7,600 seats. By offering moviegoers a radically superior experience, Kinepolis won 50% of the market in Brussels in its first year and expanded the market by about 40%. Today many Belgians refer not to a night at the movies but to an evening at Kinepolis.

Consider the differences between Kinepolis and other Belgian movie theaters. The typical Belgian multiplex has small viewing rooms that often have no more than 100 seats, screens that measure 7 meters by 5 meters, and 35-millimeter projection equipment. Viewing rooms at Kinepolis have up to 700 seats, and there is so much legroom that viewers do not have to move when someone passes by. Bert Claeys installed oversized seats with individual armrests and designed a steep slope in the floor to ensure everyone an unobstructed view. At Kinepolis, screens measure up to 29 meters by 10 meters and rest on their own foundations so that sound vibrations are not transmitted from one screen to another. Many viewing rooms have 70-millimeter projection equipment and state-of-the-art sound equipment. And Bert Claeys challenged the industry's conventional wisdom about the importance of prime, city-center real estate by locating Kinepolis off the ring road circling Brussels, 15 minutes from downtown. Patrons park for free in large, well-lit lots. The company was prepared to lose out on foot traffic in order to solve a major problem for the majority of moviegoers in Brussels: the scarcity and high cost of parking.

Bert Claeys can offer this radically superior cinema experience without increasing the price of tickets because the concept of the megaplex results in one of the lowest cost structures in the industry. The average cost to build a seat at Kinepolis is about 70,000 Belgian francs, less than half the industry's average in Brussels. Why? The megaplex's location outside the city is cheaper; its size gives it economies in purchasing, more leverage with film distributors, and better overall margins; and with 25 screens served by a central ticketing and lobby area, Kinepolis achieves economies in personnel and overhead. Furthermore, the company spends very little on advertising because its value innovation generates a lot of word-of-mouth praise.

Within its supposedly unattractive industry, Kinepolis has achieved spectacular growth and profits. Belgian moviegoers now go to the cinema more frequently because of Kinepolis, and people who never went to the movies have been drawn into the market. Instead of battling competitors over targeted segments of the market, Bert Claeys made the competition irrelevant. (See the chart "How Kinepolis Achieves Profitable Growth.")

Why did other Belgian COs fail to seize that opportunity? Like the others, Bert Claeys was an incumbent with sunk investments: a network of cinemas across Belgium. In fact, Kinepolis would have represented a smaller investment for some COs than it did for Bert Claeys. Most COs were thinking—implicitly or explicitly—along these lines: The industry is shrinking, so we should not make major investments—especially in fixed assets. But we can improve our performance by outdoing our competitors on each of the key dimensions of competition. We must have better films, better services, and better marketing.

Bert Claeys followed a different strategic logic. The company set out to make its cinema experience not better than that at competitors' theaters but completely different—and irresistible. The company thought as if it were a new entrant to the market. It sought to reach the mass of moviegoers by focusing on widely shared needs. In order to give most moviegoers a package they would value highly, the company put aside conventional thinking about what a theater is supposed to look like. And the company did all that while reducing its costs. That's the logic behind value innovation.

Conventional Logic versus Value Innovation

Conventional strategic logic and the logic of value innovation differ along the five basic dimensions of strategy. Those differences determine which questions managers ask, what opportunities they see and pursue,

How Kinepolis Achieves Profitable Growth

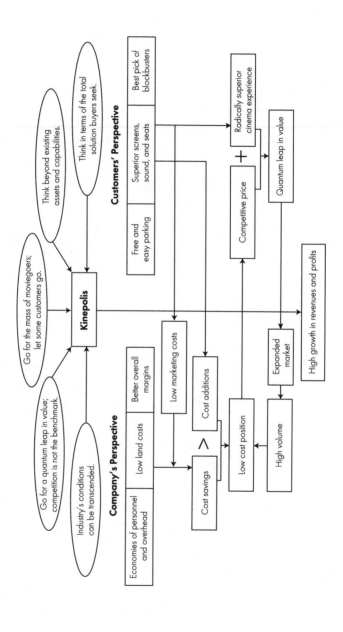

and how they understand risk. (See the table "Two Strategic Logics.")

Industry assumptions. Many companies take their industry's conditions as given and set strategy accordingly. Value innovators don't. No matter how the rest of the industry is faring, value innovators look for blockbuster ideas and quantum leaps in value. Had Bert Claeys, for example, taken its industry's conditions as given, it would never have created a megaplex. The company would have followed the endgame strategy of milking its business or the zero-sum strategy of competing for share in a shrinking market. Instead, through Kinepolis, the company transcended the industry's conditions.

Strategic focus. Many companies let competitors set the parameters of their strategic thinking. They compare their strengths and weaknesses with those of their competitors and focus on building advantages. Consider this example. For years, the major U.S. television networks used the same format for news programming. All aired shows in the same time slot and competed on their analysis of events, the professionalism with which they delivered the news, and the popularity of their anchors. In 1980, CNN came on the scene with a focus on creating a quantum leap in value, not on competing with the networks. CNN replaced the networks' format with real-time news from around the world 24 hours a day. CNN not only emerged as the leader in global news broadcasting—and created new demand around the world—but also was able to produce 24 hours of real-time news for one-fifth the cost of 1 hour of network news.

Conventional logic leads companies to compete at the margin for incremental share. The logic of value innovation starts with an ambition to dominate the market by offering a tremendous leap in value. Value innovators never say, Here's what competitors are doing; let's do this in response. They monitor competitors but do not use them as benchmarks. Hasso Plattner, vice chairman of SAP, the global leader in business-application software, puts it this way: "I'm not interested in whether we are better than the competition. The real test is, will most buyers still seek out our products even if we don't market them?"

Because value innovators do not focus on competing, they can distinguish the factors that deliver superior value from all the factors the industry competes on. They do not expend their resources to offer certain product and service features just because that is what their rivals are doing. CNN, for example, decided not to compete with the networks in the race to get big-name anchors. Companies that follow the logic of value innovation free up their resources to identify and deliver completely new sources of value. Ironically, value innovators do not set out to build advantages over the competition, but they end up achieving the greatest competitive advantages.

Customers. Many companies seek growth through retaining and expanding their customer bases. This often leads to finer segmentation and greater customization of offerings to meet specialized needs. Value innovation follows a different logic. Instead of focusing on the differences among customers, value innovators build on the powerful commonalities in the features that customers value. In the words of a senior executive at the French hotelier Accor, "We focus on what unites customers. Customers' differences often prevent you from seeing what's most important." Value innovators believe that most people will put their differences aside if they are offered a considerable increase in value. Those companies shoot for the core of the market, even if it means that they lose some of their customers.

Assets and capabilities. Many companies view business opportunities through the lens of their existing assets and capabilities. They ask, Given what we have,

Two Strategic Logics

The Five Dimensions of Strategy	Conventional Logic	Value Innovation Logic
Industry Assumptions	Industry's conditions are given.	Industry's conditions can be shaped.
Strategic Focus	A company should build competitive advantages. The aim is to beat the competition.	Competition is not the benchmark. A company should pursue a quantum leap in value to dominate the market.
Customers	A company should retain and expand its customer base through further segmentation and customization. It should focus on the differences in what customers value.	A value innovator targets the mass of buyers and willingly lets some existing customers go. It focuses on the key commonalities in what customers value.
Assets and Capabilities	A company should leverage its existing assets and capabilities.	A company must not be constrained by what it already has. It must ask, What would we do if we were starting anew?
Product and Service Offerings	An industry's traditional boundaries determine the product and services a company offers. The goal is to maximize the value of those offerings.	A value innovator thinks in terms of the total solution customers seek, even if that takes the company beyond its industry's traditional offerings.

what is the best we can do? In contrast, value innovators ask, What if we start anew? That is the question the British company Virgin Group put to itself in the late 1980s. The company had a sizable chain of small music stores across the United Kingdom when it came up with the idea of megastores for music and entertainment, which would offer customers a tremendous leap in value. Seeing that its small stores could not be leveraged to seize that opportunity, the company decided to sell off the entire chain. As one of Virgin's executive puts it, "We don't let what we can do today condition our view of what it takes to win tomorrow. We take a clean-slate approach."

This is not to say that value innovators never leverage their existing assets and capabilities. They often do. But, more important, they assess business opportunities without being biased or constrained by where they are at a given moment. For that reason, value innovators not only have more insight into where value for buyers resides—and how it is changing—but also are much more likely to act on that insight.

Product and service offerings. Conventional competition takes place within clearly established boundaries defined by the products and services the industry traditionally offers. Value innovators often cross those boundaries. They think in terms of the total solution buyers seek, and they try to overcome the chief compromises their industry forces customers to make—as Bert Claeys did by providing free parking. A senior executive at Compaq Computer describes the approach: "We continually ask where our products and services fit in the total chain of buyers' solutions. We seek to solve buyers' major problems across the entire chain, even if that takes us into a new business. We are not limited by the industry's definition of what we should and should not do."

Creating a New Value Curve

How does the logic of value innovation translate into a company's offerings in the marketplace? Consider the case of Accor. In the mid-1980s, the budget hotel industry in France was suffering from stagnation and overcapacity. Accor's cochairmen, Paul Dubrule and Gérard Pélisson, challenged the company's managers to create a quantum leap in value for customers. The managers were urged to forget everything they knew about the existing rules, practices, and traditions of the industry. They were asked what they would do if Accor were starting fresh.

In 1985, when Accor launched Formule 1, a line of budget hotels, there were two distinct market segments in the budget hotel industry. One segment consisted of no-star and one-star hotels, whose average price per room was between 60 and 90 French francs. Customers came to those hotels just for the low price. The other segment was two-star hotels, with an average price of 200 francs per room. Those more expensive hotels attracted customers by offering a better sleeping environment than the no-star and one-star hotels. People had come to expect that they would get what they paid for: either they would pay more and get a decent night's sleep or they would pay less and put up with poor beds and noise.

Accor's managers began by identifying what customers of all budget hotels—no-star, one-star, and two-star—wanted: a good night's sleep for a low price.

Focusing on those widely shared needs, Accor's managers saw the opportunity to overcome the chief compromise that the industry forced customers to make. They asked themselves the following four questions:

- Which of the factors that our industry takes for granted should be eliminated?

- Which factors should be reduced well below the industry's standard?

- Which factors should be raised well above the industry's standard?

- Which factors should be created that the industry has never offered?

The first question forces managers to consider whether the factors that companies compete on actually deliver value to consumers. Often those factors are taken for granted, even though they have no value or even detract from value. Sometimes what buyers value changes fundamentally, but companies that are focused on benchmarking one another do not act on—or even perceive—the change. The second question forces managers to determine whether products and services have been overdesigned in the race to match and beat the competition. The third question pushes managers to uncover and eliminate the compromises their industry forces customers to make. The fourth question helps managers break out of the industry's established boundaries to discover entirely new sources of value for consumers.

In answering the questions, Accor came up with a new concept for a hotel, which led to the launch of Formule 1. First, the company eliminated such standard hotel features as costly restaurants and appealing lounges. Accor reckoned that even though it might lose some customers, most people would do without those features.

Accor's managers believed that budget hotels were overserving customers along other dimensions as well. On those, Formule 1 offers less than many no-star hotels do. For example, receptionists are on hand only during peak check-in and check-out hours. At all other times, customers use an automated teller. Rooms at a Formule 1 hotel are small and equipped only with a bed and bare necessities—no stationery, desks, or decorations. Instead of closets and dressers, there are a few shelves and a pole for clothing in one corner of the room. The rooms themselves are modular blocks manufactured in a factory—a method that results in economies of scale in production, high quality control, and good sound insulation.

Formule 1 gives Accor considerable cost advantages. The company cut in half the average cost of building a room, and its staff costs dropped from between 25% and 35% of sales—the industry's average—to between 20% and 23%. Those cost savings have allowed Accor to improve the features customers value most to levels beyond those of the average French two-star hotel, but the price is only marginally above that of one-star hotels.

Customers have rewarded Accor for its value innovation. The company has not only captured the mass of French budget-hotel customers but also expanded the market. From truck drivers who previously slept in their vehicles to businesspeople needing a few hours of rest, new customers have been drawn to the budget category. Formule 1 made the competition irrelevant. At last count, Formule 1's market share in France was greater than the sum of the five next-largest players.

The extent of Accor's departure from the conventional logic of its industry can be seen in what we call a *value curve*—a graphic depiction of a company's relative performance across its industry's key success factors. (See the graph "Formule 1's Value Curve.") According to the conventional logic of competition, an industry's value curve follows one basic shape. Rivals try to improve value by offering a little more for a little less, but most don't challenge the shape of the curve.

Formule 1's Value Curve

Formule 1 offers unprecedented value to the mass of budget hotel customers in France by giving them much more of what they need most and much less of what they are willing to do without.

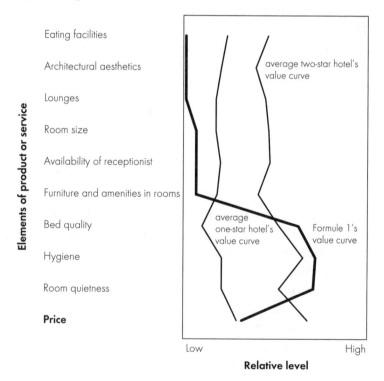

Like Accor, all the high-performing companies we studied created fundamentally new and superior value curves. They achieved that by a combination of eliminating features, creating features, and reducing and raising others to levels unprecedented in their industries. Take, for example, SAP, a business-application-software company that was started in the early 1970s by five former IBM employees in Walldorf, Germany, and became the worldwide industry leader. Until the 1980s, business-application-software makers focused on subsegmenting the market and customizing their offerings to meet buyers' functional needs, such as production management, logistics, human resources, and payroll.

While most software companies were focusing on improving the performance of particular application products, SAP took aim at the mass of buyers. Instead of competing on customers' differences, SAP sought out important commonalities in what customers value. The company correctly hypothesized that for most customers, the performance advantages of highly customized, individual software modules had been overestimated. Such modules forfeited the efficiency and information advantages of an integrated system, which allows real-time data exchange across a company.

In 1979, SAP launched R/2, a line of real-time, integrated business-application software for mainframe computers. R/2 has no restriction on the platform of the host hardware; buyers can capitalize on the best hardware available and reduce their maintenance costs dramatically. Most important, R/2 leads to huge gains in accuracy and efficiency because a company needs to enter its data only once. And R/2 improves the flow of information. A sales manager, for example, can find out when a product will be delivered and why it is late by cross-referencing the production database. SAP's growth and profits have exceeded its industry's. In 1992, SAP achieved a new value innovation with R/3, a line of software for the client-server market.

The Trap of Competing, the Necessity of Repeating

What happens once a company has created a new value curve? Sooner or later, the competition tries to imitate it. In many industries, value innovators do not face a credible challenge for many years, but in others, rivals appear more quickly. Eventually, however, a value innovator will find its growth and profits under attack. Too often, in an attempt to defend its hard-earned customer base, the company launches offenses. But the imitators often persist, and the value innovator—despite its best intentions—may end up in a race to beat the competition. Obsessed with hanging on to market share, the company may fall into the trap of conventional strategic logic. If the company doesn't find its way out of the trap, the basic shape of its value curve will begin to look just like those of its rivals.

Consider the following example. When Compaq Computer launched its first personal computer in 1983, most PC buyers were sophisticated corporate users and technology enthusiasts. IBM had defined the industry's value curve. Compaq's first offering—the first IBM-compatible PC—represented a completely new value curve. Compaq's product not only was technologically superb but also was priced roughly 15% below IBM's. Within three years of its start-up, Compaq joined the *Fortune* 500. No other company had ever achieved that status as quickly.

How did IBM respond? It tried to match and beat Compaq's value curve. And Compaq, determined to defend itself, became focused on beating IBM. But while IBM and Compaq were battling over feature enhancements, most buyers were becoming more sensitive to price. User-friendliness was becoming more important to customers than the latest technology. Compaq's focus on competing with IBM led the company to produce a line of PCs that were overengineered and overpriced for most buyers. When IBM walked off the cliff in the late 1980s, Compaq was following close behind.

Could Compaq have foreseen the need to create another value innovation rather than go head-to-head against IBM? If Compaq had monitored the industry's value curves, it would have realized that by the mid-to-late 1980s, IBM's and other PC makers' value curves were converging with its own. And by the late 1980s, the curves were nearly identical. That should have been the signal to Compaq that it was time for another quantum leap.

Monitoring value curves may also keep a company from pursuing innovation when there is still a huge profit stream to be collected from its current offering. In some rapidly emerging industries, companies must innovate frequently. In many other industries, companies can harvest their successes for a long time: a radically different value curve is difficult for incumbents to imitate, and the volume advantages that come with value innovation make imitation costly. Kinepolis, Formule 1, and CNN, for example, have enjoyed uncontested dominance for a long time. CNN's value innovation was not challenged for almost ten years. Yet we have seen companies pursue novelty for novelty's sake, driven by internal pressures to leverage unique competencies or to apply the latest technology. Value innovation is about offering unprecedented value, not technology or competencies. It is not the same as being first to market.

When a company's value curve is fundamentally different from that of the rest of the industry—and the difference is valued by most customers—managers should resist innovation. Instead, companies should embark on geographic expansion and operational improvements to achieve maximum economies of scale and market coverage. That approach discourages imitation and allows companies to tap the potential of their current value innovation. Bert Claeys, for example, has been rapidly rolling out and improving its Kinepolis concept with Metropolis, a megaplex in Antwerp, and with megaplexes in many countries in Europe and Asia. And Accor has already built more than 300 Formule 1 hotels across Europe, Africa, and Australia. The company is now targeting Asia.

The Three Platforms

The companies we studied that were most successful at repeating value innovation were those that took advantage of all three platforms on which value innovation can take place: product, service, and delivery. The precise meaning of the three platforms varies across industries and companies, but, in general, the product platform is the physical product; the service platform is support such as maintenance, customer service, warranties, and training for distributors and retailers; and the delivery platform includes logistics and the channel used to deliver the product to customers.

Too often, managers trying to create a value innovation focus on the product platform and ignore the other two. Over time, that approach is not likely to yield many opportunities for repeated value innovation. As customers and technologies change, each platform presents new possibilities. Just as good farmers rotate their crops, good value innovators rotate their value platforms. (See "Virgin Atlantic: Flying in the Face of Conventional Logic" at the end of this article.)

The story of Compaq's server business, which was part of the company's successful comeback, illustrates how the three platforms can be used alternately over time to create new value curves. (See the graph "How Has Compaq Stayed on Top of the Server Industry?") In late 1989, Compaq introduced its first server, the SystemPro, which was designed to run five network operating systems—SCO UNIX, OS/2, Vines, NetWare, and DOS—and many application programs. Like the System-Pro, most servers could handle many operating systems and application programs. Compaq observed, however, that the majority of customers used only a small fraction of a server's capacity. After identifying the needs that cut across the mass of users, Compaq decided to build a radically simplified server that would be optimized to run NetWare and file and print only. Launched in 1992, the ProSignia was a value innovation on the product platform. The new server gave buyers twice the System-Pro's file-and-print performance at one-third the price. Compaq achieved that value innovation mainly by reducing general application compatibility—a reduction that translated into much lower manufacturing costs.

As competitors tried to imitate the ProSignia and value curves in the industry began to converge, Compaq took another leap, this time from the service platform.

How Has Compaq Stayed on Top of the Server Industry?

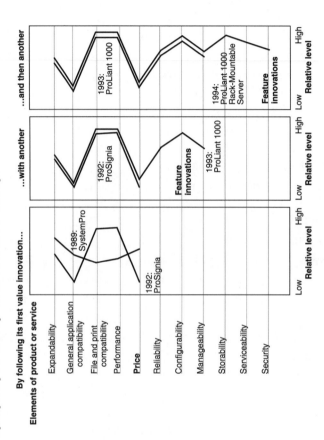

By following its first value innovation....

...with another

...and then another

Elements of product or service

- Expandability
- General application compatibility
- File and print compatibility
- Performance
- **Price**
- Reliability
- Configurability
- Manageability
- Storability
- Serviceability
- Security

1989: SystemPro

1992: ProSignia

1992: ProSignia

Feature innovations

1993: ProLiant 1000

1993: ProLiant 1000

1994: ProLiant 1000 Rack-Mountable Server

Feature innovations

Low   High
Relative level

Low   High
Relative level

Low   High
Relative level

Viewing its servers not as stand-alone products but as elements of its customers' total computing needs, Compaq saw that 90% of customers' costs were in servicing networks and only 10% were in the server hardware itself. Yet Compaq, like other companies in the industry, had been focusing on maximizing the price-performance ratio of the server hardware, the least costly element for buyers.

Compaq redeployed its resources to bring out the ProLiant 1000, a server that incorporates two innovative pieces of software. The first, SmartStart, configures server hardware and network information to suit a company's operating system and application programs. It slashes the time it takes a customer to configure a server network and makes installation virtually error-free so that servers perform reliably from day one. The second piece of software, Insight Manager, helps customers manage their server networks by, for example, spotting overheating boards or troubled disk drives before they break down.

By innovating on the service platform, Compaq created a superior value curve and expanded its market. Companies lacking expertise in information technology had been skeptical of their ability to configure and manage a network server. SmartStart and Insight Manager helped put those companies at ease. The ProLiant 1000 came out a winner.

As more and more companies acquired servers, Compaq observed that its customers often lacked the space to store the equipment properly. Stuffed into closets or left on the floor with tangled wires, expensive servers were often damaged, were certainly not secure, and were difficult to service.

By focusing on customer value—not on competitors—Compaq saw that it was time for another value innovation on the product platform. The company introduced the ProLiant 1000 Rack-Mountable Server, which allows companies to store servers in a tall, lean cabinet in a central location. The product makes efficient use of space and ensures that machines are protected and are easy to monitor, repair, and enhance. Compaq designed the rack mount to fit both its products and those of other manufacturers, thus attracting even more buyers and discouraging imitation. The company's sales and profits rose again as its new value curve diverged from the industry's.

Compaq is now looking to the delivery platform for a value innovation that will dramatically reduce the lead time between a customer's order and the arrival of the equipment. Lead times have forced customers to forecast their needs—a difficult task—and have often required them to patch together costly solutions while waiting for their orders to be filled. Now that servers are widely used and the demands placed on them are multiplying rapidly, Compaq believes that shorter lead times will provide a quantum leap in value for customers. The company is currently working on a delivery option that will permit its products to be built to customers' specifications and shipped within 48 hours of the order. That value innovation will allow Compaq to reduce its inventory costs and minimize the accumulation of outdated stock.

By achieving value innovations on all three platforms, Compaq has been able to maintain a gap between its value curve and those of other players. Despite the pace of competition in its industry, Compaq's repeated value innovations are allowing the company to remain the number one maker of servers worldwide. Since the company's turnaround, overall sales and profits have almost quadrupled.

Driving a Company for High Growth

One of the most striking findings of our research is that despite the profound impact of a company's strategic logic, that logic is often not articulated. And because it goes unstated and unexamined, a company does not necessarily apply a consistent strategic logic across its businesses.

How can senior executives promote value innovation? First, they must identify and articulate the company's prevailing strategic logic. Then they must challenge it. They must stop and think about the industry's assumptions, the company's strategic focus, and the approaches—to customers, assets and capabilities, and product and service offerings—that are taken as given. Having reframed the company's strategic logic around value innovation, senior executives must ask the four questions that translate that thinking into a new value curve: Which of the factors that our industry takes for granted should be eliminated? Which factors should be reduced well below the industry's standard? Which should be raised well above the industry's standard? What factors should be created that the industry has never offered? Asking the full set of questions—rather than singling out one or two—is necessary for profitable growth. Value innovation is the simultaneous pursuit of radically superior value for buyers and lower costs for companies.

For managers of diversified corporations, the logic of value innovation can be used to identify the most promising possibilities for growth across a portfolio of businesses. The value innovators we studied all have been pioneers in their industries, not necessarily in developing new technologies but in pushing the value they offer customers to new frontiers. Extending the pioneer metaphor can provide a useful way of talking about the growth potential of current and future businesses.

A company's *pioneers* are the businesses that offer unprecedented value. They are the most powerful sources of profitable growth. At the other extreme are *settlers*—businesses with value curves that conform to the basic shape of the industry's. Settlers will not generally contribute much to a company's growth. The potential of *migrators* lies somewhere in between. Such businesses extend the industry's curve by giving customers more for less, but they don't alter its basic shape.

Testing the Growth Potential of a Portfolio of Businesses

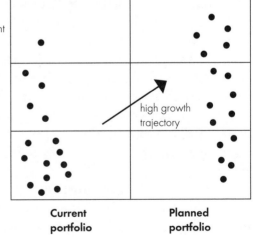

The Pioneer-Migrator-Settler Map

Pioneers
Businesses that represent value innovations

Migrators
Businesses with value improvements

high growth trajectory

Settlers
Businesses that offer me-too products and services

Current portfolio   Planned portfolio

A useful exercise for a management team pursuing growth is to plot the company's current and planned portfolios on a pioneer-migrator-settler map. (See the chart "Testing the Growth Potential of a Portfolio of Businesses.") If both the current portfolio and the planned offerings consist mainly of settlers, the company has a low growth trajectory and needs to push for value innovation. The company may well have fallen into the trap of competing. If current and planned offerings consist of a lot of migrators, reasonable growth can be expected. But the company is not exploiting its potential for growth and risks being marginalized by a value innovator. This exercise is especially valuable for managers who want to see beyond today's performance numbers. Revenue, profitability, market share, and customer satisfaction are all measures of a company's current position. Contrary to what conventional strategic thinking suggests, those measures cannot point the way to the future. The pioneer-migrator-settler map can help a company predict and plan future growth and profit, a task that is especially difficult—and crucial—in a fast-changing economy.

Researching the Roots of High Growth

OVER THE LAST FIVE YEARS, we studied more than 30 companies around the world in approximately 30 industries. We looked at companies with high growth in both revenues and profits and companies with less successful performance records. In an effort to explain the difference in performance between the two groups of companies, we interviewed hundreds of managers, analysts, and researchers. We built strategic, organizational, and performance profiles. We looked for industry or organizational patterns. And we compared the two groups of companies along dimensions that are often thought to be related to a company's potential for growth. Did private companies grow more quickly than public ones? What was the impact on companies of the overall growth of their industry? Did entrepreneurial start-ups have an edge over established incumbents? Were companies led by creative, young radicals likely to grow faster than those run by older managers?

We found that none of those factors mattered in a systematic way. High growth was achieved by both small and large organizations, by companies in high-tech and low-tech industries, by new entrants and incumbents, by private and public companies, and by companies from various countries.

What did matter—consistently—was the way managers in the two groups of companies thought about strategy. In interviewing the managers, we asked them to describe their strategic moves and the thinking behind them. Thus we came to understand their views on each of the five textbook dimensions of strategy: industry assumptions, strategic focus, customers, assets and capabilities, and product and service offerings. We were struck by what emerged from our content analysis of those interviews. The managers of the high-growth companies—irrespective of their industry—all described what we have come to call the logic of value innovation. The managers of the less successful companies all thought along conventional strategic lines.

Intrigued by that finding, we went on to test whether the managers of the high-growth companies applied their strategic thinking to business initiatives in the marketplace. We found that they did.

Furthermore, in studying the business launches of about 100 companies, we were able to quantify the impact of value innovation on a company's growth in both revenues and profits. Although 86% of the launches were line extensions—that is, incremental improvements—they accounted for 62% of total revenues and only 39% of total profits. The remaining 14% of the launches—the true value innovations—generated 38% of total revenues and a whopping 61% of total profits.

Virgin Atlantic: Flying in the Face of Conventional Logic

WHEN VIRGIN ATLANTIC AIRWAYS challenged its industry's conventional logic by eliminating first-class service in 1984, the airline was simply following the logic of value innovation. Most of the industry's profitable revenue came from business class, not first class. And first class was a big cost generator. Virgin spotted an opportunity. The airline decided to channel the cost it would save by cutting first-class service into value innovation for business-class passengers.

First, Virgin introduced large, reclining sleeper seats, raising seat comfort in business class well above the industry's standard. Second, Virgin offered free transportation to and from the airport—initially in chauffeured limousines and later in specially designed motorcycles called LimoBikes—to speed business-class passengers through snarled city traffic.

With those innovations, which were on the product and service platforms, Virgin attracted not only a large share of the industry's business-class customers but also some full-economy-fare and first-class passengers of other airlines. Virgin's value innovation separated the company from the pack for many years, but the competition did not stand still. As the value curves of some other airlines began converging with Virgin's value curve, the company went for another leap in value, this time from the service platform.

Virgin observed that most business-class passengers want to use their time productively before and between flights and that, after long-haul flights, they want to freshen up and change their wrinkled clothes before going to meetings. The airline designed lounges where passengers can have their clothes pressed, take showers, enjoy massages, and use state-of-the-art office equipment. The service allows busy executives to make good use of their time and go directly to meetings without first stopping at their hotels—a tremendous value for customers that generates high volume for Virgin. The airline has one of the highest sales per employee in the industry, and its costs per passenger mile are among the lowest. The economics of value innovation create a positive and reinforcing cycle.

When Virgin first challenged the industry's assumptions, its ideas were met with a great deal of skepticism. After all, conventional wisdom says that in order to grow, a company must embrace *more*, not fewer, market segments. But Virgin deliberately walked away from the revenue generated by first-class passengers. And it further violated conventional wisdom by conceiving of its business in terms of customer solutions, even if that took the company well beyond an airline's traditional offerings.

Virgin has applied the logic of value innovation not just to the airline industry but also to insurance and to music and entertainment retailing. Virgin has always done more than leverage its existing assets and capabilities. The company has been a consistent value innovator.

Originally published in January–February 1997
Reprint 97108

About the Contributors

TERESA M. AMABILE holds the MBA Class of 1954 Chair as Professor of Business Administration at the Harvard Business School. Originally focusing on individual creativity, Dr. Amabile's research has expanded to encompass team creativity and organizational innovation. Her current work centers on how specific events in organizations and project teams can influence team members' work environment, motivation, creativity, and productivity. Dr. Amabile is the author of *Creativity in Context* and *Growing up Creative,* as well as over 100 scholarly papers, chapters, and presentations.

PETER F. DRUCKER is a writer, teacher, and consultant whose thirty-one books have been published in more than twenty languages. He is the cofounder of the Peter F. Drucker Foundation for Nonprofit Management, and has counseled numerous governments, public service institutions, and major corporations. In addition, Mr. Drucker has published more than thirty articles in the *Harvard Business Review,* has been a frequent contributor to magazines such as *The Atlantic Monthly,* and was a columnist for the *Wall Street Journal* from 1975 to 1995.

W. CHAN KIM is the Boston Consulting Group Bruce D. Henderson Chair Professor of Strategy and International Management at INSEAD and Fellow of the World Economic

Forum at Davos. Prior to joining INSEAD, he was a professor at the University of Michigan Business School. He has published numerous articles on strategy and managing the multinational in *Academy of Management Journal, Management Science, Organization Science, Strategic Management Journal, Journal of International Business Studies, Sloan Management Review, Harvard Business Review,* and others. He is also a contributor to the *Wall Street Journal,* the *Wall Street Journal Europe,* the *Financial Times,* the *New York Times,* and the *International Herald Tribune.*

DOROTHY LEONARD holds the William J. Abernathy Professor of Business Administration chair at the Harvard Business School, where she has taught in MBA and executive education programs since 1983. She researches and consults about innovation, new-product development, and the transfer of knowledge across geographic, cultural, and cognitive boundaries. Professor Leonard has published dozens of articles based on field research in academic journals such as *Organization Science.* She is the author of *Wellspring of Knowledge* (HBS Press, 1995) and the coauthor with Walter Swap of the forthcoming book *When Sparks Fly: Igniting Creativity in Groups* (HBS Press, 1999).

RICHARD K. LESTER is the founder and director of the Massachusetts Institute of Technology Industrial Performance Center and a professor of nuclear engineering at MIT. Dr. Lester's research focuses on strategies for innovation, productivity, and industrial competition. He is the author of *The Productive Edge: How American Industries are Pointing the Way to a New Era of Economic Growth* (W. W. Norton, 1998), and the coauthor of *Made by Hong Kong* (Oxford University Press, 1997) and *Made in America: Regaining the Productive Edge* (MIT Press, 1989), the best-selling report of the MIT Commission on Industrial Productivity. Professor Lester serves as an advisor to corporations, governments, and non-profit groups, and lectures frequently to academic, business, and general audiences throughout the world.

KAMAL M. MALEK is a Ph.D. candidate at the Massachusetts Institute of Technology. He holds S.B. and S.M. degrees in mechanical engineering, also from MIT. His current research, under the direction of MIT Professors Richard K. Lester and Michael J. Piore, focuses on problems of internal and external integration in situations of radical uncertainty, as typified by new-product development projects. Mr. Malek has several years of work experience in the automotive industry and, more recently, has consulted for a number of corporations, including a game developer, a software startup, and a construction and real estate development company, in the areas of engineering and management.

RENÉE MAUBORGNE is the INSEAD Distinguished Fellow and Affiliate Professor of Strategy and Management at INSEAD and Fellow of the World Economic Forum at Davos. She is also president of ITM Research, a research group committed to discovering ideas that matter in the knowledge economy. She has published numerous articles on strategy and managing the multinational in *Academy of Management Journal, Management Science, Organization Science, Strategic Management Journal, Journal of International Business Studies, Sloan Management Review, Harvard Business Review*, and others. She is also a contributor to the *Wall Street Journal*, the *Financial Times*, the *New York Times*, and the *International Herald Tribune*.

At the time her article was published in the *Harvard Business Review*, EILEEN MORLEY was a psychologist teaching at the Harvard Business School. Her main interests concerned the organization of work and the personal satisfaction people derive from their careers.

MICHAEL J. PIORE is the David W. Skinner Professor of Political Economy at MIT and Associate Director of the Center for Technology Policy and Industrial Development. As a labor economist, he is best known for developing the concept of the internal labor market and the dual labor market hypothesis and, more recently, for work on the transition from mass production to flexible specialization. He is the author of numerous short papers and journal articles, as well as several books, including *Beyond Individualism* (Harvard University Press, 1995); *The Second Industrial Divide* (Basic Books, 1984), written in collaboration with Charles Sabel; *Birds of Passage* (Cambridge University Press, 1979); *Unemployment and Inflation* (Sharpe Press, 1979); *Dualism and Discontinuity in Economic Life,* with Suzanne Berger (Cambridge University Press, 1980); and *Internal Labor Markets and Manpower Analysis* (Cambridge University Press, 1969), with Peter Doeringer.

JEFFREY F. RAYPORT is an Associate Professor of Business Administration in the Service Management Unit at the Harvard Business School. His research investigates the impact of new information technologies on service management and marketing strategies for business, with a focus on digital commerce in information-based and knowledge-intensive industries. As a consultant, Dr. Rayport has worked with corporations and professional practices in North and South America, Europe, Japan, and the Pacific Rim. His consulting work helps companies develop breakthrough service strategies in network-based or digital sectors of the economy.

Before completing the research described in his article for his doctorate degree from the Harvard Business School in 1975, ANDREW SILVER taught film at Brandeis University. At the time the article was published, he had made two short films, one of which, *Next Door,* won a Blue Ribbon at the American Film Festival in 1976.

SUSAAN STRAUS is a management consultant and speaker who specializes in organizational change and management team effectiveness. Her research, involving thousands of managers and executives in *Fortune* 500 companies, has focused on the effect of cognitive preference and on the abilities of leaders, managers, and teams as they face the challenges of the need to innovate in a rapidly changing workplace. An experienced conflict mediator and process facilitator, she resides in Newton, Massachusetts, and Nogolas, Chile. She leads Performance Resources, whose mission is to elicit excellent performance in organizations committed to transformation and renewal.

SUZY WETLAUFER, formerly of the international management consulting firm Bain & Company, is a senior editor at the *Harvard Business Review*, specializing in the area of organization. In addition to "The Team That Wasn't," she is the author of several other *Harvard Business Review* pieces, including "Organizing for Empowerment: An Interview with AES's Roger Sant and Dennis Bakke" and, with Charles M. Farkas, "Ways Chief Executive Officers Lead."

Note: *Information provided within each article about the contributors to case studies and perspectives was applicable at the time of original publication.*

Index